P9-CCH-542

Tamburlaine

DOVER · THRIFT · EDITIONS

Tamburlaine

CHRISTOPHER MARLOWE

DOVER PUBLICATIONS, INC.
Mineola, New York

DOVER THRIFT EDITIONS

GENERAL EDITOR: PAUL NEGRI
EDITOR OF THIS VOLUME: THOMAS CRAWFORD

Copyright

Copyright © 2002 by Dover Publications, Inc.
All rights reserved under Pan American and International Copyright Conventions.

Published in Canada by General Publishing Company, Ltd., 895 Don Mills Road, 400-2 Park Centre, Toronto, Ontario M3C 1W3.
Published in the United Kingdom by David & Charles, Brunel House, Forde Close, Newton Abbot, Devon TQ12 4PU.

Bibliographical Note

This Dover edition, first published in 2002, is a republication of the text of *Tamburlaine the Great*, Parts 1 and 2, as published in *Christopher Marlowe*, a volume in The Mermaid Series, edited by Havelock Ellis, and published by Vizetelly & Co., London, 1887. A new introductory Note has been specially prepared for this edition.

Library of Congress Cataloging-in-Publication Data

Marlowe, Christopher, 1564–1593.
Tamburlaine / Christopher Marlowe.
p. cm.
ISBN 0-486-42125-2 (pbk.)
1. Timur, 1336–1405—Drama. 2. Asia, Central—Drama. 3. Conquerors—Drama. I. Title.

PR2669 .A1 2002
822'.3—dc21

2002017526

Manufactured in the United States of America
Dover Publications, Inc., 31 East 2nd Street, Mineola, N.Y. 11501

Note

POET, SPY, barroom brawler, and the greatest Elizabethan playwright before Shakespeare, Christopher Marlowe (1564–1593) was the eldest son of a shoemaker. Born in Canterbury in 1564, just two months before the Bard, he graduated with an M. A. from Cambridge in 1587. He then went to London, where he became an actor and dramatist for the Lord Admiral's company. There is also some indication that he may have worked as a secret agent for the government. In 1593, he was stabbed to death in a tavern in Deptford by one of his companions, perhaps in an argument over the bill. Because of Marlowe's apparent double life as a spy, however, some feel he may have been provoked and murdered to prevent him from implicating others.

Despite his untimely death and the consequent truncation of his literary career, Marlowe was an extraordinarily influential figure. Swinburne called him "the father of English tragedy and the creator of English blank verse," while Tennyson wrote: "If Shakespeare is the dazzling sun of this mighty period, Marlowe is certainly the morning star." His influence rests partly on his position as a founder of English drama and on the power, beauty, and dignity of his blank verse—"Marlowe's mighty line" in the words of Ben Jonson. In pioneering and perfecting this new form of dramatic poesy, Marlowe in a very real sense paved the way for one greater than himself—William Shakespeare. And while Marlowe's plays are often full of passion, violence, and bloodshed, it is the transcendent poetic language and imagery of his plays that lifts them to the level of high art.

Tamburlaine the Great, Marlowe's first play, was first performed in London ca. 1587. Comprised of two parts of five acts each, it was an immediate and enduring success with Elizabethan playgoers, who applauded what Nash called the "swelling bombast" of the play's blank verse, and the intensely imaginative form in which Marlowe clothed the dry bones of the story. Like Marlowe's other plays *(The Jew of*

Malta, Dr. Faustus, Edward II), the drama centers on a strong central character, dominated by an all-consuming passion. In the case of Tamburlaine, that passion is for power. The play is based on an actual historical figure, the Mongol conqueror Timur or Tamerlane (1336–1405), a Scythian shepherd who subdued vast areas of Russia, Persia, India, and Central Persia, and was planning an invasion of China when he died.

In Marlowe's hands, Tamburlaine is at first a figure of intense romanticism, one that undoubtedly appealed to the bold spirit of the Elizabethan age. Fearless, ambitious, and charismatic, he sweeps all before him, routing opposing armies and establishing a vast empire. Although a warrior, Tamburlaine is also a thinker who muses in poetic terms on the powerful attraction of earthly goals:

> Our souls, whose faculties can comprehend
> The wondrous architecture of the world
> And measure every wandering planet's course,
> Still climbing after knowledge infinite,
> And always moving as the restless sphere,
> Will us to wear ourselves, and never rest,
> Until we reach the ripest fruit of all,
> That perfect bliss and sole felicity,
> The Sweet fruition of an earthly crown.

At the end of Part I, Tamburlaine basks in the glory of his "earthly crown." However, the conqueror's poetic side is less and less in evidence in Part II, as further conquests are achieved through treachery and an ever-widening trail of atrocities. By the end of the play, Tamburlaine's inhuman cruelty, arrogance, and over-arching lust for power have branded him one of history's greatest tyrants. Despite his many enemies, however, in the end he is brought down not by military foes, but by sickness, perhaps divine punishment for the unparalleled hubris that led him to call himself "the Scourge of God."

Tamburlaine

PART THE FIRST

The Prologue

From jigging veins of rhyming mother wits,
And such conceits as clownage keeps in pay,
We'll lead you to the stately tent of war,
Where you shall hear the Scythian Tamburlaine
Threatening the world with high astounding terms,
And scourging kingdoms with his conquering sword.
View but his picture in this tragic glass,
And then applaud his fortune as you please.

Dramatis Personæ

MYCETES, King of Persia.
COSROE, his Brother.

ORTYGIUS, CENEUS, MEANDER, MENAPHON, THERIDAMAS,	Persian Lords and Captains.

TAMBURLAINE, a Scythian Shepherd.

TECHELLES, USUMCASANE,	his Followers.

BAJAZETH, Emperor of the Turks.
KING OF ARABIA.
KING of FEZ.
KING of MOROCCO.
KING of ARGIER (Algiers).
SOLDAN of EGYPT.
GOVERNOR of DAMASCUS.

AGYDAS, MAGNETES,	Median Lords.

CAPOLIN, an Egyptian Captain.
PHILEMUS, a Messenger.

ZENOCRATE, Daughter of the Soldan of Egypt.
ANIPPE, her Maid.
ZABINA, Wife of Bajazeth.
EBEA, her Maid.
Virgins of Damascus.

No list of the characters is given in the early editions; the omission is frequent in plays of this period.

ACT THE FIRST

SCENE I.

Enter MYCETES, COSROE, MEANDER, THERIDAMAS, ORTYGIUS, CENEUS, MENAPHON, *with others.*

MYC. Brother Cosroe, I find myself aggrieved,
Yet insufficient to express the same;
For it requires a great and thundering speech:
Good brother, tell the cause unto my lords;
I know you have a better wit than I.
COS. Unhappy Persia, that in former age
Hast been the seat of mighty conquerors,
That, in their prowess and their policies,
Have triumphed over Afric and the bounds
Of Europe, where the sun scarce dares appear
For freezing meteors and congealèd cold,
Now to be ruled and governed by a man
At whose birthday Cynthia with Saturn joined,
And Jove, the Sun, and Mercury denied
To shed their influence in his fickle brain!
Now Turks and Tartars shake their swords at thee,
Meaning to mangle all thy provinces.
MYC. Brother, I see your meaning well enough,
And through your planets I perceive you think
I am not wise enough to be a king;
But I refer me to my noblemen
That know my wit, and can be witnesses.
I might command you to be slain for this:
Meander, might I not?
MEAND. Not for so small a fault, my sovereign lord.
MYC. I mean it not, but yet I know I might;
Yet live; yea live, Mycetes wills it so.
Meander, thou, my faithful counsellor,

Declare the cause of my conceivèd grief,
Which is, God knows, about that Tamburlaine,
That, like a fox in midst of harvest time,
Doth prey upon my flocks of passengers;
And, as I hear, doth mean to pull my plumes:
Therefore 'tis good and meet for to be wise.

MEAND. Oft have I heard your majesty complain
Of Tamburlaine, that sturdy Scythian thief,
That robs your merchants of Persepolis
Trading by land unto the Western Isles,
And in your confines with his lawless train
Daily commits incivil[1] outrages,
Hoping (misled by dreaming prophecies)
To reign in Asia, and with barbarous arms
To make himself the monarch of the East;
But ere he march in Asia, or display
His vagrant ensign in the Persian fields,
Your grace hath taken order by Theridamas,
Charged with a thousand horse, to apprehend
And bring him captive to your highness' throne.

MYC. Full true thou speak'st, and like thyself, my lord,
Whom I may term a Damon for thy love:
Therefore 'tis best, if so it like you all,
To send my thousand horse incontinent[2]
To apprehend that paltry Scythian.
How like you this, my honourable lords?
Is't not a kingly resolution?

COS. It cannot choose, because it comes from you.

MYC. Then hear thy charge, valiant Theridamas,
The chiefest captain of Mycetes' host,
The hope of Persia, and the very legs
Whereon our State doth lean as on a staff
That holds us up, and foils our neighbour foes:
Thou shalt be leader of this thousand horse,
Whose foaming gall with rage and high disdain
Have sworn the death of wicked Tamburlaine.
Go frowning forth; but come thou smiling home,
As did Sir Paris with the Grecian dame;
Return with speed—time passeth swift away;
Our life is frail, and we may die to-day.

---

1 Brutal.
2 Forthwith.

THER. Before the moon renew her borrowed light,
Doubt not, my lord and gracious sovereign,
But Tamburlaine and that Tartarian rout,
Shall either perish by our warlike hands,
Or plead for mercy at your highness' feet.
MYC. Go, stout Theridamas, thy words are swords,
And with thy looks thou conquerest all thy foes;
I long to see thee back return from thence,
That I may view these milk-white steeds of mine
All loaden with the heads of killèd men,
And from their knees e'en to their hoofs below
Besmeared with blood that makes a dainty show.
THER. Then now, my lord, I humbly take my leave.
MYC. Theridamas, farewell! ten thousand times.
[*Exit* THERIDAMAS.
Ah, Menaphon, why stay'st thou thus behind,
When other men press forward for renown?
Go, Menaphon, go into Scythia;
And foot by foot follow Theridamas.
COS. Nay, pray you let him stay; a greater task
Fits Menaphon than warring with a thief:
Create him Prorex[3] of all Africa,
That he may win the Babylonians' hearts
Which will revolt from Persian government,
Unless they have a wiser king than you.
MYC. "Unless they have a wiser king than you."
These are his words; Meander, set them down.
COS. And add this to them—that all Asia
Laments to see the folly of their king.
MYC. Well, here I swear by this my royal seat,—
COS. You may do well to kiss it then.
MYC. Embossed with silk as best beseems my state,
To be revenged for these contemptuous words.
Oh, where is duty and allegiance now?
Fled to the Caspian or the Ocean main?
What shall I call thee? brother?—no, a foe;
Monster of nature!—shame unto thy stock
That dar'st presume thy sovereign for to mock!
Meander, come: I am abused, Meander.
[*Exeunt all but* COSROE *and* MENAPHON.

3 Viceroy.

MEN. How now, my lord? What, mated[4] and amazed
To hear the king thus threaten like himself!
COS. Ah, Menaphon, I pass not[5] for his threats;
The plot is laid by Persian noblemen
And captains of the Median garrisons
To crown me Emperor of Asia:
But this it is that doth excruciate
The very substance of my vexèd soul—
To see our neighbours that were wont to quake
And tremble at the Persian monarch's name,
Now sit and laugh our regiment[6] to scorn;
And that which might resolve[7] me into tears,
Men from the farthest equinoctial line
Have swarmed in troops into the Eastern India,
Lading their ships with gold and precious stones,
And made their spoils from all our provinces.
MEN. This should entreat your highness to rejoice,
Since Fortune gives you opportunity
To gain the title of a conqueror
By curing of this maimèd empery.
Afric and Europe bordering on your land,
And continent to your dominions,
How easily may you, with a mighty host,
Pass into Græcia, as did Cyrus once,
And cause them to withdraw their forces home,
Lest you subdue the pride of Christendom.
[*Trumpet within.*
COS. But, Menaphon, what means this trumpet's sound?
MEN. Behold, my lord, Ortygius and the rest
Bringing the Crown to make you Emperor!

Enter ORTYGIUS *and* CENEUS, *with others, bearing a crown.*

ORTY. Magnificent and mighty Prince Cosroe,
We, in the name of other Persian States[8]
And Commons of the mighty monarchy,
Present thee with the imperial diadem.
CEN. The warlike soldiers and the gentlemen,
That heretofore have filled Persepolis

4 Confounded.
5 Care not.
6 Rule.
7 Dissolve.
8 *i.e.*, Persons of state.

With Afric captains taken in the field,
Whose ransom made them march in coats of gold,
With costly jewels hanging at their ears,
And shining stones upon their lofty crests,
Now living idle in the wallèd towns,
Wanting both pay and martial discipline,
Begin in troops to threaten civil war,
And openly exclaim against their king:
Therefore, to stop all sudden mutinies,
We will invest your highness Emperor,
Whereat the soldiers will conceive more joy
Than did the Macedonians at the spoil
Of great Darius and his wealthy host.

COS. Well, since I see the state of Persia droop
And languish in my brother's government,
I willingly receive the imperial crown,
And vow to wear it for my country's good,
In spite of them shall malice[9] my estate.

ORTY. And in assurance of desired success,
We here do crown thee monarch of the East,
Emperor of Asia and Persia;
Great Lord of Media and Armenia;
Duke of Africa and Albania,
Mesopotamia and of Parthia,
East India and the late-discovered isles;
Chief Lord of all the wide, vast Euxine sea,
And of the ever-raging Caspian lake.

ALL. Long live Cosroe, mighty Emperor!

COS. And Jove may never let me longer live[10]
Than I may seek to gratify your love,
And cause the soldiers that thus honour me
To triumph over many provinces!
By whose desire of discipline in arms
I doubt not shortly but to reign sole king,
And with the army of Theridamas,
(Whither we presently will fly, my lords)
To rest secure against my brother's force.

ORTY. We knew, my lord, before we brought the crown,
Intending your investion so near

9 "Malice" was frequently used as a verb.

10 Meaning "And may Jove," &c. Marlowe had very vague ideas respecting the Persian and Mahommedan religions. Tamburlaine often invokes Jove, and seems to be well versed in the Greek mythology.

The residence of your despisèd brother,
The lords would not be too exasperate
To injury[11] or suppress your worthy title;
Or, if they would, there are in readiness
Ten thousand horse to carry you from hence,
In spite of all suspected enemies.
COS. I know it well, my lord, and thank you all.
ORTY. Sound up the trumpets then. [*Trumpets sound.*
ALL. God save the King! [*Exeunt.*

SCENE II.

Enter TAMBURLAINE *leading* ZENOCRATE, TECHELLES, USUMCASANE, AGYDAS, MAGNETES, LORDS, *and* SOLDIERS, *laden with treasure.*

TAMB. Come, lady, let not this appal your thoughts;
The jewels and the treasure we have ta'en
Shall be reserved, and you in better state,
Than if you were arrived in Syria,
Even in the circle of your father's arms,
The mighty Soldan of Ægyptia.
ZENO. Ah, shepherd! pity my distressèd plight,
(If, as thou seem'st, thou art so mean a man),
And seek not to enrich thy followers
By lawless rapine from a silly maid,
Who travelling with these Median lords
To Memphis, from my uncle's country of Media,
Where all my youth I have been governèd,
Have passed the army of the mighty Turk,
Bearing his privy signet and his hand
To safe conduct us thorough Africa.
MAG. And since we have arrived in Scythia,
Besides rich presents from the puissant Cham,
We have his highness' letters to command
Aid and assistance, if we stand in need.
TAMB. But now you see these letters and commands
Are countermanded by a greater man;
And through my provinces you must expect
Letters of conduct from my mightiness,
If you intend to keep your treasure safe.
But, since I love to live at liberty,

11 "Injury," like "malice," was sometimes used as a verb by early writers.

As easily may you get the Soldan's crown
As any prizes out of my precinct;
For they are friends that help to wean my state
'Till men and kingdoms help to strengthen it,
And must maintain my life exempt from servitude.—
But, tell me, madam, is your grace betrothed?
ZENO. I am—my lord—for so you do import.
TAMB. I am a lord, for so my deeds shall prove:
And yet a shepherd by my parentage.
But, lady, this fair face and heavenly hue
Must grace his bed that conquers Asia,
And means to be a terror to the world,
Measuring the limits of his empery
By east and west, as Phœbus doth his course.
Lie here, ye weeds that I disdain to wear!
This complete armour and this curtle-axe[1]
Are adjuncts more beseeming Tamburlaine.
And, madam, whatsoever you esteem
Of this success, and loss unvaluèd,[2]
Both may invest you Empress of the East;
And these that seem but silly country swains
May have the leading of so great an host,
As with their weight shall make the mountains quake,
Even as when windy exhalations
Fighting for passage, tilt within the earth.
TECH. As princely lions, when they rouse themselves,
Stretching their paws, and threatening herds of beasts,
So in his armour looketh Tamburlaine.
Methinks I see kings kneeling at his feet,
And he with frowning brows and fiery looks,
Spurning their crowns from off their captive heads.
USUM. And making thee and me, Techelles, kings,
That even to death will follow Tamburlaine.
TAMB. Nobly resolved, sweet friends and followers!
These lords, perhaps do scorn our estimates,
And think we prattle with distempered spirits;
But since they measure our deserts so mean,
That in conceit bear empires on our spears,
Affecting thoughts coequal with the clouds,

1 The curtle-axe (Fr. *coutelasse*) was not an axe, but a short curved sword, which survives in the modern cutlass.
2 Invaluable.

They shall be kept our forcèd followers,
Till with their eyes they view us emperors.
ZENO. The gods, defenders of the innocent,
Will never prosper your intended drifts,
That thus oppress poor friendless passengers.
Therefore at least admit us liberty,
Even as thou hopest to be eternised,
By living Asia's mighty Emperor.
AGYD. I hope our ladies' treasure and our own,
May serve for ransom to our liberties:
Return our mules and empty camels back,
That we may travel into Syria,
Where her betrothèd lord Alcidamas,
Expects th' arrival of her highness' person.
MAG. And wheresoever we repose ourselves,
We will report but well of Tamburlaine.
TAMB. Disdains Zenocrate to live with me?
Or you, my lords, to be my followers?
Think you I weigh this treasure more than you?
Not all the gold in India's wealthy arms
Shall buy the meanest soldier in my train.
Zenocrate, lovelier than the love of Jove,
Brighter than is the silver Rhodope,
Fairer than whitest snow on Scythian hills,—
Thy person is more worth to Tamburlaine,
Than the possession of the Persian crown,
Which gracious stars have promised at my birth.
A hundred Tartars shall attend on thee,
Mounted on steeds swifter than Pegasus;
Thy garments shall be made of Median silk,
Enchased with precious jewels of mine own,
More rich and valurous[3] than Zenocrate's.
With milk-white harts upon an ivory sled,
Thou shalt be drawn amidst the frozen pools,
And scale the icy mountains' lofty tops,
Which with thy beauty will be soon resolved.
My martial prizes with five hundred men,
Won on the fifty-headed Volga's waves,
Shall we all offer to Zenocrate,—
And then myself to fair Zenocrate.
TECH. What now!—in love?

3 Valuable.

TAMB. Techelles, women must be flatterèd:
But this is she with whom I am in love.

Enter a Soldier.

SOLD. News! news!
TAMB. How now—what's the matter?
SOLD. A thousand Persian horsemen are at hand,
Sent from the king to overcome us all.
TAMB. How now, my lords of Egypt, and Zenocrate!
How!—must your jewels be restored again,
And I, that triumphed so, be overcome?
How say you, lordlings,—is not this your hope?
AGYD. We hope yourself will willingly restore them.
TAMB. Such hope, such fortune, have the thousand horse.
Soft ye, my lords, and sweet Zenocrate!
You must be forcèd from me ere you go.
A thousand horsemen!—We five hundred foot!—
An odds too great for us to stand against.
But are they rich?—And is their armour good?
SOLD. Their plumèd helms are wrought with beaten gold,
Their swords enamelled, and about their necks
Hang massy chains of gold, down to the waist,
In every part exceeding brave[4] and rich.
TAMB. Then shall we fight courageously with them?
Or look you I should play the orator?
TECH. No: cowards and faint-hearted runaways
Look for orations when the foe is near:
Our swords shall play the orator for us.
USUM. Come! let us meet them at the mountain top,
And with a sudden and a hot alarum,
Drive all their horses headlong down the hill.
TECH. Come, let us march!
TAMB. Stay, Techelles! ask a parley first.

The Soldiers *Enter.*

Open the mails,[5] yet guard the treasure sure;
Lay out our golden wedges to the view,
That their reflections may amaze the Persians;
And look we friendly on them when they come;

4 Fine.
5 Trunks. Fr. *malles.*

But if they offer word or violence,
We'll fight five hundred men-at-arms to one,
Before we part with our possession.
And 'gainst the general we will lift our swords,
And either lance his greedy thirsting throat,
Or take him prisoner, and his chain shall serve
For manacles, till he be ransomed home.

TECH. I hear them come; shall we encounter them?

TAMB. Keep all your standings and not stir a foot,
Myself will bide the danger of the brunt.

Enter THERIDAMAS *and others.*

THER. Where is this Scythian Tamburlaine?

TAMB. Whom seek'st thou, Persian?—I am Tamburlaine.

THER. Tamburlaine!—
A Scythian shepherd so embellishèd
With nature's pride and richest furniture!
His looks do menace Heaven and dare the gods:
His fiery eyes are fixed upon the earth,
As if he now devised some stratagem,
Or meant to pierce Avernus' darksome vaults
To pull the triple-headed dog from hell.

TAMB. Noble and mild this Persian seems to be,
If outward habit judge the inward man.

TECH. His deep affections make him passionate.

TAMB. With what a majesty he rears his looks!
In thee, thou valiant man of Persia,
I see the folly of thy emperor.
Art thou but captain of a thousand horse,
That by charàcters graven in thy brows,
And by thy martial face and stout aspèct,
Deserv'st to have the leading of a host!
Forsake thy king, and do but join with me,
And we will triumph over all the world;
I hold the Fates bound fast in iron chains,
And with my hand turn Fortune's wheel about:
And sooner shall the sun fall from his sphere,
Than Tamburlaine be slain or overcome.
Draw forth thy sword, thou mighty man-at-arms,
Intending but to raze my charmèd skin,
And Jove himself will stretch his hand from Heaven
To ward the blow and shield me safe from harm.
See how he rains down heaps of gold in showers,

As if he meant to give my soldiers pay!
And as a sure and grounded argument,
That I shall be the monarch of the East,
He sends this Soldan's daughter rich and brave,
To be my Queen and portly Emperess.
If thou wilt stay with me, renownèd man,
And lead thy thousand horse with my condúct,
Besides thy share of this Egyptian prize,
Those thousand horse shall sweat with martial spoil
Of conquered kingdoms and of cities sacked;
Both we will walk upon the lofty cliffs,
And Christian merchants[6] that with Russian stems
Plough up huge furrows in the Caspian sea,
Shall vail[7] to us, as lords of all the lake.
Both we will reign as consuls of the earth,
And mighty kings shall be our senators.
Jove sometimes maskèd in a shepherd's weed,
And by those steps that he hath scaled the Heavens
May we become immortal like the gods.
Join with me now in this my mean estate,
(I call it mean because being yet obscure,
The nations far removed admire me not),
And when my name and honour shall be spread
As far as Boreas claps his brazen wings,
Or fair Böotes sends his cheerful light,
Then shalt thou be competitor[8] with me,
And sit with Tamburlaine in all his majesty.

THER. Not Hermes, prolocutor to the gods,
Could use persuasions more pathetical.

TAMB. Nor are Apollo's oracles more true,
Than thou shalt find my vaunts substantial.

TECH. We are his friends, and if the Persian king
Should offer present dukedoms to our state,
We think it loss to make exchange for that
We are assured of by our friend's success.

USUM. And kingdoms at the least we all expect,
Besides the honour in assurèd conquests,
When kings shall crouch unto our conquering swords
And hosts of soldiers stand amazed at us;

---

6 Merchantmen.
7 Lower their flags.
8 Associate.

When with their fearful tongues they shall confess,
These are the men that all the world admires.

THER. What strong enchantments tice my yielding soul!
These resolvèd, noble Scythians:
But shall I prove a traitor to my king?

TAMB. No, but the trusty friend of Tamburlaine.

THER. Won with thy words, and conquered with thy looks,
I yield myself, my men, and horse to thee,
To be partaker of thy good or ill,
As long as life maintains Theridamas.

TAMB. Theridamas, my friend, take here my hand,
Which is as much as if I swore by Heaven,
And called the gods to witness of my vow.
Thus shall my heart be still combined with thine
Until our bodies turn to elements,
And both our souls aspire celestial thrones.
Techelles and Casane, welcome him!

TECH. Welcome, renownèd Persian, to us all!

USUM. Long may Theridamas remain with us!

TAMB. These are my friends, in whom I more rejoice
Than doth the King of Persia in his crown,
And by the love of Pylades and Orestes,
Whose statues we adore in Scythia,
Thyself and them shall never part from me
Before I crown you kings in Asia.
Make much of them, gentle Theridamas,
And they will never leave thee till the death.

THER. Nor thee nor them, thrice noble Tamburlaine,
Shall want my heart to be with gladness pierced,
To do you honour and security.

TAMB. A thousand thanks, worthy Theridamas.
And now fair madam, and my noble lords,
If you will willingly remain with me
You shall have honours as your merits be;
Or else you shall be forced with slavery.

AGYD. We yield unto thee, happy Tamburlaine.

TAMB. For you then, madam, I am out of doubt.

ZENO. I must be pleased perforce. Wretched Zenocrate!

[*Exeunt.*

ACT THE SECOND.

SCENE I.

Enter COSROE, MENAPHON, ORTYGIUS, *and* CENEUS, *with* Soldiers.

COS. Thus far are we towards Theridamas,
And valiant Tamburlaine, the man of fame,
The man that in the forehead of his fortune
Bears figures of renown and miracle.
But tell me, that hast seen him, Menaphon,
What stature wields he, and what personage?
MEN. Of stature tall, and straightly fashionèd,
Like his desire lift upward and divine;
So large of limbs, his joints so strongly knit,
Such breadth of shoulders as might mainly bear
Old Atlas' burthen;—'twixt his manly pitch,[1]
A pearl, more worth than all the world, is placed,
Wherein by curious sovereignty of art
Are fixed his piercing instruments of sight,
Whose fiery circles bear encompassèd
A heaven of heavenly bodies in their spheres,
That guides his steps and actions to the throne,
Where honour sits invested royally:
Pale of complexion, wrought in him with passion,
Thirsting with sovereignty and love of arms;
His lofty brows in folds do figure death,
And in their smoothness amity and life;
About them hangs a knot of amber hair,
Wrappèd in curls, as fierce Achilles' was,
On which the breath of Heaven delights to play,

1 Originally the height to which a falcon soared; hence for height in general. Here it means the shoulders.

Making it dance with wanton majesty.—
His arms and fingers, long, and sinewy,
Betokening valour and excess of strength;—
In every part proportioned like the man
Should make the world subdued to Tamburlaine.
COS. Well hast thou pourtrayed in thy terms of life
The face and personage of a wondrous man;
Nature doth strive with Fortune and his stars
To make him famous in accomplished worth;
And well his merits show him to be made
His fortune's master and the king of men,
That could persuade at such a sudden pinch,
With reasons of his valour and his life,
A thousand sworn and overmatching foes.
Then, when our powers in points of swords are joined
And closed in compass of the killing bullet,
Though strait the passage and the port[2] be made
That leads to palace of my brother's life,
Proud is his fortune if we pierce it not.
And when the princely Persian diadem
Shall overweigh his weary witless head,
And fall like mellowed fruit with shakes of death,
In fair Persia, noble Tamburlaine
Shall be my regent and remain as king.
ORTY. In happy hour we have set the crown
Upon your kingly head that seeks our honour,
In joining with the man ordained by Heaven,
To further every action to the best.
CEN. He that with shepherds and a little spoil
Durst, in disdain of wrong and tyranny,
Defend his freedom 'gainst a monarchy,
What will he do supported by a king,
Leading a troop of gentlemen and lords,
And stuffed with treasure for his highest thoughts!
COS. And such shall wait on worthy Tamburlaine.
Our army will be forty thousand strong,
When Tamburlaine and brave Theridamas
Have met us by the river Araris;
And all conjoined to meet the witless king,
That now is marching near to Parthia,
And with unwilling soldiers faintly armed,

---

2 Gate.

To seek revenge on me and Tamburlaine,
To whom, sweet Menaphon, direct me straight.
MEN. I will, my lord. [*Exeunt.*

SCENE II.

Enter MYCETES, MEANDER, *with other* Lords *and* Soldiers.

MYC. Come, my Meander, let us to this gear.
I tell you true, my heart is swoln with wrath
On this same thievish villain, Tamburlaine,
And on that false Cosroe, my traitorous brother.
Would it not grieve a king to be so abused
And have a thousand horsemen ta'en away?
And, which is worse, to have his diadem
Sought for by such scald[1] knaves as love him not?
I think it would; well then, by Heavens I swear,
Aurora shall not peep out of her doors,
But I will have Cosroe by the head,
And kill proud Tamburlaine with point of sword.
Tell you the rest, Meander: I have said.
MEAND. Then having passed Armenian deserts now,
And pitched our tents under the Georgian hills,
Whose tops are covered with Tartarian thieves,
That lie in ambush, waiting for a prey,
What should we do but bid them battle straight,
And rid the world of those detested troops?
Lest, if we let them linger here awhile,
They gather strength by power of fresh supplies.
This country swarms with vile outrageous men
That live by rapine and by lawless spoil,
Fit soldiers for the wicked Tamburlaine;
And he that could with gifts and promises
Inveigle him that led a thousand horse,
And make him false his faith unto his king,
Will quickly win such as be like himself.
Therefore cheer up your minds; prepare to fight;
He that can take or slaughter Tamburlaine
Shall rule the province of Albania:
Who brings that traitor's head, Theridamas,

1 Scurvy.

Shall have a government in Media,
Beside the spoil of him and all his train:
But if Cosroe, (as our spials[2] say,
And as we know) remains with Tamburlaine,
His highness' pleasure is that he should live,
And be reclaimed with princely lenity.

A SPY. An hundred horsemen of my company
Scouting abroad upon these champion[3] plains,
Have viewed the army of the Scythians,
Which make report it far exceeds the king's.

MEAND. Suppose they be in number infinite,
Yet being void of martial discipline,
All running headlong after greedy spoils,
And more regarding gain than victory,
Like to the cruel brothers of the earth,
Sprung of the teeth of dragons venomous,
Their careless swords shall lance their fellows' throats,
And make us triumph in their overthrow.

MYC. Was there such brethren, sweet Meander, say,
That sprung of teeth of dragons venomous?

MEAND. So poets say, my lord.

MYC. And 'tis a pretty toy to be a poet.
Well, well, Meander, thou art deeply read,
And having thee, I have a jewel sure.
Go on, my lord, and give your charge, I say;
Thy wit will make us conquerors to-day.

MEAND. Then, noble soldiers, to entrap these thieves,
That live confounded in disordered troops,
If wealth or riches may prevail with them,
We have our camels laden all with gold,
Which you that be but common soldiers
Shall fling in every corner of the field;
And while the base-born Tartars take it up,
You, fighting more for honour than for gold,
Shall massacre those greedy-minded slaves;
And when their scattered army is subdued,
And you march on their slaughtered carcases,
Share equally the gold that bought their lives,
And live like gentlemen in Persia.

---

2 Spies.
3 The old way of spelling "champaign," Fr. *champagne*.

Strike up the drum! and march courageously!
Fortune herself doth sit upon our crests.
MYC. He tells you true, my masters: so he does.
Drums, why sound ye not, when Meander speaks?
[*Exeunt, drums sounding.*

SCENE III.

Enter COSROE, TAMBURLAINE, THERIDAMAS, TECHELLES, USUMCASANE, *and* ORTYGIUS, *with others.*

COS. Now, worthy Tamburlaine, have I reposed
In thy approvèd fortunes all my hope.
What think'st thou, man, shall come of our attempts?
For even as from assurèd oracle,
I take thy doom for satisfaction.
TAMB. And so mistake you not a whit, my lord;
For fates and oracles of Heaven have sworn
To royalise the deeds of Tamburlaine,
And make them blest that share in his attempts.
And doubt you not but, if you favour me,
And let my fortunes and my valour sway
To some direction in your martial deeds,
The world will strive with hosts of men-at-arms,
To swarm unto the ensign I support:
The host of Xerxes, which by fame is said
To have drank the mighty Parthian Araris,
Was but a handful to that we will have.
Our quivering lances, shaking in the air,
And bullets, like Jove's dreadful thunderbolts,
Enrolled in flames and fiery smoldering mists,
Shall threat the gods more than Cyclopian wars:
And with our sun-bright armour as we march,
We'll chase the stars from Heaven and dim their eyes
That stand and muse at our admirèd arms.
THER. You see, my lord, what working words he hath;
But when you see his actions top his speech,
Your speech will stay or so extol his worth
As I shall be commended and excused
For turning my poor charge to his direction.
And these his two renownèd friends, my lord,
Would make one thirst and strive to be retained
In such a great degree of amity.

TECH. With duty and with amity we yield
Our utmost service to the fair Cosroe.
COS. Which I esteem as portion of my crown.
Usumcasane and Techelles both,
When she that rules in Rhamnus'[1] golden gates,
And makes a passage for all prosperous arms,
Shall make me solely Emperor of Asia,
Then shall your meeds and valours be advanced
To rooms of honour and nobility.
TAMB. Then haste, Cosroe, to be king alone,
That I with these, my friends, and all my men
May triumph in our long-expected fate.—
The king, your brother, is now hard at hand;
Meet with the fool, and rid your royal shoulders
Of such a burthen as outweighs the sands
And all the craggy rocks of Caspia.

Enter a Messenger.

MES. My lord, we have discovered the enemy
Ready to charge you with a mighty army.
COS. Come, Tamburlaine! now whet thy wingèd sword,
And lift thy lofty arm into the clouds,
That it may reach the King of Persia's crown,
And set it safe on my victorious head.
TAMB. See where it is, the keenest curtle-axe
That e'er made passage thorough Persian arms.
These are the wings shall make it fly as swift
As doth the lightning or the breath of Heaven,
And kill as sure as it swiftly flies.
COS. Thy words assure me of kind success;
Go, valiant soldier, go before and charge
The fainting army of that foolish king.
TAMB. Usumcasane and Techelles, come!
We are enow to scare the enemy,
And more than needs to make an emperor.
[*Exeunt to the battle.*

---

1 The allusion is to Nemesis, who had a temple at Rhamnus in Attica.

Scene IV.

Enter Myceates *with his crown in his hand.*

Myc. Accursed be he that first invented war!
They knew not, ah they knew not, simple men,
How those were hit by pelting cannon shot,
Stand staggering like a quivering aspen leaf
Fearing the force of Boreas' boisterous blasts.
In what a lamentable case were I
If Nature had not given me wisdom's lore,
For kings are clouts that every man shoots at,
Our crown the pin[1] that thousands seek to cleave;
Therefore in policy I think it good
To hide it close; a goodly stratagem,
And far from any man that is a fool:
So shall I not be known; or if I be,
They cannot take away my crown from me.
Here will I hide it in this simple hole.

Enter Tamburlaine.

Tamb. What, fearful coward, straggling from the camp,
When kings themselves are present in the field?
Myc. Thou liest.
Tamb. Base villain! darest give me the lie?
Myc. Away; I am the king; go; touch me not.
Thou break'st the law of arms, unless thou kneel
And cry me "mercy, noble king."
Tamb. Are you the witty King of Persia?
Myc. Ay, marry am I: have you any suit to me?
Tamb. I would entreat you speak but three wise words.
Myc. So I can when I see my time.
Tamb. Is this your crown?
Myc. Ay, didst thou ever see a fairer?
Tamb. You will not sell it, will you?
Myc. Such another word and I will have thee executed.
Come, give it me!
Tamb. No; I took it prisoner.
Myc. You lie; I gave it you.
Tamb. Then 'tis mine.

---

1 The "clout" was the white mark in the butts at which the archers aimed, and the "pin" was the peg in the centre which fastened it.

MYC. No; I mean I let you keep it.
TAMB. Well; I mean you shall have it again.
Here; take it for a while: I lend it thee,
'Till I may see thee hemmed with armèd men;
Then shalt thou see me pull it from thy head:
Thou art no match for mighty Tamburlaine.

[*Exit* TAMBURLAINE.

MYC. O gods! Is this Tamburlaine the thief?
I marvel much he stole it not away.
[*Trumpets sound to the battle, and he runs out.*

SCENE V

Enter COSROE, TAMBURLAINE, MEANDER, THERIDAMAS, ORTYGIUS, MENAPHON, TECHELLES, USUMCASANE, *with others.*

TAMB. Hold thee, Cosroe! wear two imperial crowns;
Think thee invested now as royally,
Even by the mighty hand of Tamburlaine,
As if as many kings as could encompass thee
With greatest pomp, had crowned thee emperor.
COS. So do I, thrice renownèd man-at-arms,
And none shall keep the crown but Tamburlaine.
Thee do I make my regent of Persia,
And general lieutenant of my armies.
Meander, you, that were our brother's guide,
And chiefest counsellor in all his acts,
Since he is yielded to the stroke of war,
On your submission we with thanks excuse,
And give you equal place in our affairs.
MEAND. Most happy Emperor, in humblest terms,
I vow my service to your majesty,
With utmost virtue of my faith and duty.
COS. Thanks, good Meander: then, Cosroe, reign,
And govern Persia in her former pomp!
Now send embassage to thy neighbour kings,
And let them know the Persian king is changed,
From one that knew not what a king should do,
To one that can command what 'longs thereto.
And now we will to fair Persepolis,
With twenty thousand expert soldiers.

The lords and captains of my brother's camp
With little slaughter take Meander's course,
And gladly yield them to my gracious rule.
Ortygius and Menaphon, my trusty friends,
Now will I gratify your former good,
And grace your calling with a greater sway.

ORTY. And as we ever aimed at your behoof,
And sought your state all honour it deserved,
So will we with our powers and our lives
Endeavour to preserve and prosper it.

COS. I will not thank thee, sweet Ortygius;
Better replies shall prove my purposes.
And now, Lord Tamburlaine, my brother's camp
I leave to thee and to Theridamas,
To follow me to fair Persepolis.
Then will we march to all those Indian mines,
My witless brother to the Christians lost,
And ransom them with fame and usury.
And till thou overtake me, Tamburlaine,
(Staying to order all the scattered troops),
Farewell, lord regent and his happy friends!
I long to sit upon my brother's throne.

MEAND. Your majesty shall shortly have your wish,
And ride in triumph through Persepolis.

[*Exeunt all but* TAMBURLAINE, THERIDAMAS,
TECHELLES, *and* USUMCASANE.

TAMB. "And ride in triumph through Persepolis!"
Is it not brave to be a king, Techelles?
Usumcasane and Theridamas,
Is it not passing brave to be a king,
"And ride in triumph through Persepolis?"

TECH. O, my lord, 'tis sweet and full of pomp.

USUM. To be a king is half to be a god.

THER. A god is not so glorious as a king.
I think the pleasure they enjoy in Heaven,
Cannot compare with kingly joys in earth.—
To wear a crown enchased with pearl and gold,
Whose virtues carry with it life and death;
To ask and have, command and be obeyed;
When looks breed love, with looks to gain the prize,
Such power attractive shines in princes' eyes!

TAMB. Why say, Theridamas, wilt thou be a king?

THER. Nay, though I praise it, I can live without it.
TAMB. What say my other friends? Will you be kings?
TECH. I, if I could, with all my heart, my lord.
TAMB. Why, that's well said, Techelles; so would I,
And so would you, my masters, would you not?
USUM. What then, my lord?
TAMB. Why then, Casane, shall we wish for aught
The world affords in greatest novelty,
And rest attemptless, faint and destitute?
Methinks we should not: I am strongly moved,
That if I should desire the Persian crown,
I could attain it with a wondrous ease.
And would not all our soldiers soon consent,
If we should aim at such a dignity?
THER. I know they would with our persuasions.
TAMB. Why then, Theridamas, I'll first assay
To get the Persian kingdom to myself;
Then thou for Parthia; they for Scythia and Media;
And, if I prosper, all shall be as sure
As if the Turk, the Pope, Afric and Greece,
Came creeping to us with their crowns apace.
TECH. Then shall we send to this triumphing king,
And bid him battle for his novel crown?
USUM. Nay, quickly then, before his room be hot.
TAMB. 'Twill prove a pretty jest, in faith, my friends.
THER. A jest to charge on twenty thousand men!
I judge the purchase[1] more important far.
TAMB. Judge by thyself, Theridamas, not me;
For presently Techelles here shall haste
To bid him battle ere he pass too far,
And lose more labour than the gain will quite.[2]
Then shalt thou see the Scythian Tamburlaine,
Make but a jest to win the Persian crown.
Techelles, take a thousand horse with thee,
And bid him turn him back to war with us,
That only made him king to make us sport.
We will not steal upon him cowardly,
But give him warning and more warriors.
Haste thee, Techelles, we will follow thee.

[*Exit* TECHELLES.

1 Plunder or loot.
2 Requite.

What saith Theridamas?
THER. Go on for me. [*Exeunt.*

SCENE VI

Enter COSROE, MEANDER, ORTYGIUS, MENAPHON, *with* Soldiers.

COS. What means this devilish shepherd to aspire
With such a giantly presumption
To cast up hills against the face of Heaven,
And dare the force of angry Jupiter?
But as he thrust them underneath the hills,
And pressed out fire from their burning jaws,
So will I send this monstrous slave to hell,
Where flames shall ever feed upon his soul.
MEAND. Some powers divine, or else infernal, mixed
Their angry seeds at his conception;
For he was never sprung of human race,
Since with the spirit of his fearful pride,
He dares so doubtlessly resolve of rule,
And by profession be ambitious.
ORTY. What god, or fiend, or spirit of the earth,
Or monster turnèd to a manly shape,
Or of what mould or mettle he be made,
What star or fate soever govern him,
Let us put on our meet encountering minds;
And in detesting such a devilish thief,
In love of honour and defence of right,
Be armed against the hate of such a foe,
Whether from earth, or hell, or Heaven, he grow.
COS. Nobly resolved, my good Ortygius;
And since we all have sucked one wholesome air,
And with the same proportion of elements
Resolve, I hope we are resembled
Vowing our loves to equal death and life.
Let's cheer our soldiers to encounter him,
That grievous image of ingratitude,
That fiery thirster after sovereignty,
And burn him in the fury of that flame,
That none can quench but blood and empery.
Resolve, my lords and loving soldiers, now
To save your king and country from decay.
Then strike up, drum; and all the stars that make

The loathsome circle of my dated life,
Direct my weapon to his barbarous heart,
That thus opposeth him against the gods,
And scorns the powers that govern Persia.
[*Exeunt; drums and trumpets sounding.*

SCENE VII

Alarms of battle within. Enter COSROE, *wounded,* TAMBURLAINE, THERIDAMAS, TECHELLES, USUMCASANE, *with others.*

COS. Barbarous and bloody Tamburlaine,
Thus to deprive me of my crown and life!
Treacherous and false Theridamas,
Even at the morning of my happy state,
Scarce being seated in my royal throne,
To work my downfall and untimely end!
An uncouth pain torments my grievèd soul,
And death arrests the organ of my voice,
Who, entering at the breach thy sword hath made,
Sacks every vein and artier[1] of my heart.
Bloody and insatiate Tamburlaine!

TAMB. The thirst of reign and sweetness of a crown
That caused the eldest son of heavenly Ops,
To thrust his doting father from his chair,
And place himself in the empyreal Heaven,
Moved me to manage arms against thy state.
What better precedent than mighty Jove?
Nature that framed us of four elements,
Warring within our breasts for regiment,[2]
Doth teach us all to have aspiring minds:
Our souls, whose faculties can comprehend
The wondrous architecture of the world,
And measure every wandering planet's course,
Still climbing after knowledge infinite,
And always moving as the restless spheres,
Will us to wear ourselves, and never rest,
Until we reach the ripest fruit of all,
That perfect bliss and sole felicity,
The sweet fruition of an earthly crown.

---

1 Artery.
2 Rule.

THER. And that made me to join with Tamburlaine:
For he is gross and like the massy earth,
That moves not upwards, nor by princely deeds
Doth mean to soar above the highest sort.
TECH. And that made us the friends of Tamburlaine,
To lift our swords against the Persian king.
USUM. For as when Jove did thrust old Saturn down,
Neptune and Dis gained each of them a crown,
So do we hope to reign in Asia,
If Tamburlaine be placed in Persia.
COS. The strangest men that ever nature made!
I know not how to take their tyrannies.
My bloodless body waxeth chill and cold,
And with my blood my life slides through my wound;
My soul begins to take her flight to hell,
And summons all my senses to depart.—
The heat and moisture, which did feed each other,
For want of nourishment to feed them both,
Are dry and cold; and now doth ghastly death,
With greedy talons gripe my bleeding heart,
And like a harpy tirès[3] on my life.
Theridamas and Tamburlaine, I die:
And fearful vengeance light upon you both!
[COSROE dies.—TAMBURLAINE *takes his crown and puts it on.*
TAMB. Not all the curses which the Furies breathe,
Shall make me leave so rich a prize as this.
Theridamas, Techelles, and the rest,
Who think you now is King of Persia?
ALL. Tamburlaine! Tamburlaine!
TAMB. Though Mars himself, the angry god of arms,
And all the earthly potentates conspire
To dispossess me of this diadem,
Yet will I wear it in despite of them,
As great commander of this eastern world,
If you but say that Tamburlaine shall reign.
ALL. Long live Tamburlaine and reign in Asia!
TAMB. So now it is more surer on my head,
Than if the gods had held a parliament,
And all pronounced me King of Persia.
[*Exeunt.*

3 Preys. A term in falconry.

ACT THE THIRD.

SCENE I.

Enter BAJAZETH, *the* KINGS *of* FEZ, MOROCCO, *and* ARGIER,[1] *with others in great pomp.*

BAJ. Great Kings of Barbary and my portly bassoes,[2]
We hear the Tartars and the eastern thieves,
Under the conduct of one Tamburlaine,
Presume a bickering with your emperor,
And think to rouse us from our dreadful siege
Of the famous Grecian Constantinople.
You know our army is invincible;
As many circumcisèd Turks we have,
And warlike bands of Christians renied,[3]
As hath the ocean or the Terrene sea[4]
Small drops of water when the moon begins
To join in one her semicircled horns.
Yet would we not be braved with foreign power,
Nor raise our siege before the Grecians yield,
Or breathless lie before the city walls.
K. OF FEZ. Renownèd Emperor, and mighty general,
What, if you sent the bassoes of your guard
To charge him to remain in Asia,
Or else to threaten death and deadly arms
As from the mouth of mighty Bajazeth.
BAJ. Hie thee, my basso, fast to Persia,
Tell him thy Lord, the Turkish Emperor,

---

1 Algiers.
2 Bashaws or Pashas.
3 Christians who have abjured their faith. Fr. *renier*.
4 The Mediterranean.

Dread Lord of Afric, Europe, and Asia,
Great King and conqueror of Græcia,
The ocean, Terrene, and the Coal-black sea,[5]
The high and highest monarch of the world
Wills and commands (for say not I entreat),
Not once to set his foot on Africa,
Or spread his colours once in Græcia,
Lest he incur the fury of my wrath.
Tell him I am content to take a truce,
Because I hear he bears a valiant mind:
But if, presuming on his silly power,
He be so mad to manage arms with me,
Then stay thou with him; say, I bid thee so:
And if, before the sun have measured Heaven
With triple circuit, thou regreet us not,
We mean to take his morning's next arise
For messenger he will not be reclaimed,
And mean to fetch thee in despite of him.

BAS. Most great and puissant monarch of the earth,
Your basso will accomplish your behest,
And show your pleasure to the Persian,
As fits the legate of the stately Turk. [*Exit.*

K. OF ARG. They say he is the King of Persia;
But, if he dare attempt to stir your siege,
'Twere requisite he should be ten times more,
For all flesh quakes at your magnificence.

BAJ. True, Argier; and trembles at my looks.

K. OF MOR. The spring is hindered by your smothering host,
For neither rain can fall upon the earth,
Nor sun reflex his virtuous beams thereon,
The ground is mantled with such multitudes.

BAJ. All this is true as holy Mahomet;
And all the trees are blasted with our breaths.

K. OF FEZ. What thinks your greatness best to be achieved
In pursuit of the city's overthrow?

BAJ. I will the captive pioners of Argier
Cut off the water that by leaden pipes
Runs to the city from the mountain Carnon.
Two thousand horse shall forage up and down,

---

5 The Black Sea.

That no relief or succour come by land:
And all the sea my galleys countermand.
Then shall our footmen lie within the trench,
And with their cannons mouthed like Orcus' gulf,
Batter the walls, and we will enter in;
And thus the Grecians shall be conquerèd. [*Exeunt.*

SCENE II.

Enter ZENOCRATE, AGYDAS, ANIPPE, *with others.*

AGYD. Madam Zenocrate, may I presume
To know the cause of these unquiet fits,
That work such trouble to your wonted rest?
'Tis more than pity such a heavenly face
Should by heart's sorrow wax so wan and pale,
When your offensive rape by Tamburlaine,
(Which of your whole displeasures should be most),
Hath seemed to be digested long ago.
ZENO. Although it be digested long ago,
As his exceeding favours have deserved,
And might content the Queen of Heaven, as well
As it hath changed my first conceived disdain,
Yet since a farther passion feeds my thoughts
With ceaseless and disconsolate conceits,
Which dyes my looks so lifeless as they are,
And might, if my extremes had full events,
Make me the ghastly counterfeit of death.
AGYD. Eternal heaven sooner be dissolved,
And all that pierceth Phœbus' silver eye,
Before such hap fall to Zenocrate!
ZENO. Ah, life and soul, still hover in his breast,
And leave my body senseless as the earth.
Or else unite you to his life and soul,
That I may live and die with Tamburlaine!

Enter, behind, TAMBURLAINE, TECHELLES, *and others.*

AGYD. With Tamburlaine! Ah, fair Zenocrate,
Let not a man so vile and barbarous,
That holds you from your father in despite,
And keeps you from the honours of a queen,
(Being supposed his worthless concubine),
Be honoured with your love but for necessity.

So, now the mighty Soldan hears of you,
Your highness needs not doubt but in short time
He will with Tamburlaine's destruction
Redeem you from this deadly servitude.

ZENO. Agydas leave to wound me with these words,
And speak of Tamburlaine as he deserves.
The entertainment we have had of him
Is far from villainy[1] or servitude,
And might in noble minds be counted princely.

AGYD. How can you fancy one that looks so fierce,
Only disposed to martial stratagems?
Who, when he shall embrace you in his arms,
Will tell how many thousand men he slew;
And when you look for amorous discourse,
Will rattle forth his facts[2] of war and blood,
Too harsh a subject for your dainty ears.

ZENO. As looks the Sun through Nilus' flowing stream,
Or when the Morning holds him in her arms,
So looks my lordly love, fair Tamburlaine;
His talk much sweeter than the Muses' song
They sung for honour 'gainst Pierides,
Or when Minerva did with Neptune strive:
And higher would I rear my estimate
Than Juno, sister to the highest god,
If I were matched with mighty Tamburlaine.

AGYD. Yet be not so inconstant in your love;
But let the young Arabian live in hope
After your rescue to enjoy his choice.
You see though first the King of Persia,
Being a shepherd, seemed to love you much,
Now in his majesty he leaves those looks,
Those words of favour, and those comfortings,
And gives no more than common courtesies.

ZENO. Thence rise the tears that so distain my cheeks
Fearing his love through my unworthiness.—

[TAMBURLAINE *goes to her and takes her away lovingly by the hand, looking wrathfully on* AGYDAS. *Exeunt* all but AGYDAS.

AGYD. Betrayed by fortune and suspicious love,
Threatened with frowning wrath and jealousy,

---

1 Subjection.
2 Deeds.

Surprised with fear of hideous revenge,
I stand aghast; but most astonièd[3]
To see his choler shut in secret thoughts,
And wrapt in silence of his angry soul.
Upon his brows was pourtrayed ugly death;
And in his eyes the furies of his heart
That shine as comets, menacing revenge,
And cast a pale complexion on his cheeks.
As when the seaman sees the Hyades
Gather an army of Cimmerian clouds,
(Auster and Aquilon with wingèd steeds,
All sweating, tilt about the watery Heavens,
With shivering spears enforcing thunder claps,
And from their shields strike flames of lightning),
All-fearful folds his sails and sounds the main,
Lifting his prayers to the Heavens for aid
Against the terror of the winds and waves,
So fares Agydas for the late-felt frowns
That sent a tempest to my daunted thoughts,
And make my soul divine her overthrow.

Re-enter TECHELLES *with a naked dagger, followed by* USUMCASANE.

TECH. See you, Agydas, how the king salutes you?
He bids you prophesy what it imports.
AGYD. I prophesied before, and now I prove
The killing frowns of jealousy and love.
He needed not with words confirm my fear,
For words are vain where working tools present
The naked action of my threatened end:
It says, Agydas, thou shalt surely die,
And of extremities elect the least;
More honour and less pain it may procure
To die by this resolvèd hand of thine,
Than stay the torments he and Heaven have sworn.
Then haste, Agydas, and prevent the plagues
Which thy prolongèd fates may draw on thee.
Go, wander, free from fear of tyrant's rage,
Removèd from the torments and the hell,
Wherewith he may excruciate thy soul,

3 Astonished.

And let Agydas by Agydas die,
And with this stab slumber eternally. [*Stabs himself.*
TECH. Usumcasane, see, how right the man
Hath hit the meaning of my lord, the king.
USUM. 'Faith, and Techelles, it was manly done;
And since he was so wise and honourable,
Let us afford him now the bearing hence,
And crave his triple-worthy burial.
TECH. Agreed, Casane; we will honour him.
[*Exeunt bearing out the body.*

SCENE III.

Enter TAMBURLAINE, TECHELLES, USUMCASANE, THERIDAMAS, *a* Basso, ZENOCRATE, ANIPPE, *with others.*

TAMB. Basso, by this thy lord and master knows
I mean to meet him in Bithynia:
See how he comes! tush, Turks are full of brags,
And menace more than they can well perform.
He meet me in the field, and fetch thee hence!
Alas! poor Turk! his fortune is too weak
To encounter with the strength of Tamburlaine.
View well my camp, and speak indifferently;
Do not my captains and my soldiers look
As if they meant to conquer Africa?
BAS. Your men are valiant, but their number few,
And cannot terrify his mighty host.
My lord, the great commander of the world,
Besides fifteen contributory kings,
Hath now in arms ten thousand Janissaries,
Mounted on lusty Mauritanian steeds,
Brought to the war by men of Tripoli;
Two hundred thousand footmen that have served
In two set battles fought in Græcia;
And for the expedition of this war,
If he think good, can from his garrisons
Withdraw as many more to follow him.
TECH. The more he brings the greater is the spoil,
For when they perish by our warlike hands,
We mean to set our footmen on their steeds,
And rifle all those stately Janisars.
TAMB. But will those kings accompany your lord?

BAS. Such as his highness please; but some must stay
To rule the provinces he late subdued.
TAMB. [*To his* Officers.] Then fight courageously: their crowns are yours;
This hand shall set them on your conquering heads,
That made me Emperor of Asia.
USUM. Let him bring millions infinite of men,
Unpeopling Western Africa and Greece,
Yet we assure us of the victory.
THER. Even he that in a trice vanquished two kings,
More mighty than the Turkish emperor,
Shall rouse him out of Europe, and pursue
His scattered army till they yield or die.
TAMB. Well said, Theridamas; speak in that mood;
For *will* and *shall* best fitteth Tamburlaine,
Whose smiling stars give him assurèd hope
Of martial triumph ere he meet his foes.
I that am termed the scourge and wrath of God,
The only fear and terror of the world,
Will first subdue the Turk, and then enlarge
Those Christian captives, which you keep as slaves,
Burthening their bodies with your heavy chains,
And feeding them with thin and slender fare;
That naked row about the Terrene sea,
And when they chance to rest or breathe a space,
Are punished with bastones[4] so grievously,
That they lie panting on the galley's side,
And strive for life at every stroke they give.
These are the cruel pirates of Argier,
That damnèd train, the scum of Africa,
Inhabited with straggling runagates,
That make quick havoc of the Christian blood;
But as I live that town shall curse the time
That Tamburlaine set foot in Africa.

Enter BAJAZETH *with his* Bassoes, *the* KINGS *of* FEZ, MOROCCO, *and* ARGIER, ZABINA *and* EBEA.

BAJ. Bassoes and Janissaries of my guard,
Attend upon the person of your lord,
The greatest potentate of Africa.

4 Sticks. Ital. *bastone*.

TAMB. Techelles, and the rest, prepare your swords;
I mean to encounter with that Bajazeth.
BAJ. Kings of Fez, Morocco, and Argier,
He calls me Bajazeth, whom you call lord!
Note the presumption of this Scythian slave!
I tell thee, villain, those that lead my horse,
Have to their names titles of dignity,
And dar'st thou bluntly call me Bajazeth?
TAMB. And know, thou Turk, that those which lead my horse,
Shall lead thee captive thorough Africa;
And dar'st thou bluntly call me Tamburlaine?
BAJ. By Mahomet my kinsman's sepulchre,
And by the holy Alcoran I swear,
He shall be made a chaste and lustless eunuch,
And in my sarell[5] tend my concubines;
And all his captains that thus stoutly stand,
Shall draw the chariot of my emperess,
Whom I have brought to see their overthrow.
TAMB. By this my sword, that conquered Persia,
Thy fall shall make me famous through the world.
I will not tell thee how I'll handle thee,
But every common soldier of my camp
Shall smile to see thy miserable state.
K. OF FEZ. What means the mighty Turkish emperor,
To talk with one so base as Tamburlaine?
K. OF MOR. Ye Moors and valiant men of Barbary,
How can ye suffer these indignities?
K. OF ARG. Leave words, and let them feel your lances' points
Which glided through the bowels of the Greeks.
BAJ. Well said, my stout contributory kings:
Your threefold army and my hugy[6] host
Shall swallow up these base-born Persians.
TECH. Puissant, renowned, and mighty Tamburlaine,
Why stay we thus prolonging of their lives?
THER. I long to see those crowns won by our swords,
That we may rule as kings of Africa.
USUM. What coward would not fight for such a prize?
TAMB. Fight all courageously, and be you kings;
I speak it, and my words are oracles.

5 Seraglio. Fr. *serail*.
6 Huge.

BAJ. Zabina, mother of three braver boys
Than Hercules, that in his infancy
Did pash[7] the jaws of serpents venomous;
Whose hands are made to gripe a warlike lance,
Their shoulders broad for complete armour fit,
Their limbs more large, and of a bigger size,
Than all the brats ysprung from Typhon's loins;
Who, when they come unto their father's age,
Will batter turrets with their manly fists;—
Sit here upon this royal chair of state,
And on thy head wear my imperial crown,
Until I bring this sturdy Tamburlaine,
And all his captains bound in captive chains.
ZAB. Such good success happen to Bajazeth!
TAMB. Zenocrate, the loveliest maid alive,
Fairer than rocks of pearl and precious stone,
The only paragon of Tamburlaine,
Whose eyes are brighter than the lamps of Heaven,
And speech more pleasant than sweet harmony!
That with thy looks canst clear the darkened sky,
And calm the rage of thundering Jupiter,
Sit down by her, adornèd with my crown,
As if thou wert the Empress of the world.
Stir not, Zenocrate, until thou see
Me march victoriously with all my men,
Triumphing over him and these his kings;
Which I will bring as vassals to thy feet;
Till then take thou my crown, vaunt of my worth,
And manage words with her, as we will arms.
ZENO. And may my love the King of Persia,
Return with victory and free from wound!
BAJ. Now shalt thou feel the force of Turkish arms,
Which lately made all Europe quake for fear.
I have of Turks, Arabians, Moors, and Jews,
Enough to cover all Bithynia.
Let thousands die; their slaughtered carcasses
Shall serve for walls and bulwarks to the rest
And as the heads of Hydra, so my power,
Subdued, shall stand as mighty as before.
If they should yield their necks unto the sword,

7 Dash to pieces.

Thy soldiers' arms could not endure to strike
So many blows as I have heads for thee.
Thou know'st not, foolish hardy Tamburlaine,
What 'tis to meet me in the open field,
That leave no ground for thee to march upon.

TAMB. Our conquering swords shall marshal us the way
We use to march upon the slaughtered foe,
Trampling their bowels with our horses' hoofs;
Brave horses bred on th' white Tartarian hills;
My camp is like to Julius Cæsar's host,
That never fought but had the victory;
Nor in Pharsalia was there such hot war,
As these, my followers, willingly would have.
Legions of spirits fleeting[8] in the air
Direct our bullets and our weapons' points,
And make your strokes to wound the senseless lure,[9]
And when she sees our bloody colours spread,
Then Victory begins to take her flight,
Resting herself upon my milk-white tent?—
But come, my lords, to weapons let us fall;
The field is ours, the Turk, his wife and all.

[*Exit with his followers.*

BAJ. Come, kings and bassoes, let us glut our swords,
That thirst to drink the feeble Persians' blood.

[*Exit with his followers.*

ZAB. Base concubine, must thou be placed by me,
That am the empress of the mighty Turk?

ZENO. Disdainful Turkess, and unreverend boss!
Call'st thou me concubine, that am betrothed
Unto the great and mighty Tamburlaine?

ZAB. To Tamburlaine, the great Tartarian thief!

ZENO. Thou wilt repent these lavish words of thine,
When thy great basso-master and thyself
Must plead for mercy at his kingly feet,
And sue to me to be your advocate.

ZAB. And sue to thee!—I tell thee, shameless girl,
Thou shalt be laundress to my waiting maid!
How lik'st thou her, Ebea?—Will she serve?

EBEA. Madam, perhaps, she thinks she is too fine,

---

8 Floating

9 Here "lure" most probably means "light" (Fr. *lueur*), but may refer to a decoy used to call young hawks.

But I shall turn her into other weeds,
And make her dainty fingers fall to work,

ZENO. Hear'st thou, Anippe, how thy drudge doth talk?
And how my slave, her mistress, menaceth?
Both for their sauciness shall be employed
To dress the common soldiers' meat and drink,
For we will scorn they should come near ourselves.

ANIP. Yet sometimes let your highness send for them
To do the work my chambermaid disdains.

[They sound to the battle within.

ZENO. Ye gods and powers that govern Persia,
And made my lordly love her worthy king,
Now strengthen him against the Turkish Bajazeth,
And let his foes, like flocks of fearful roes
Pursued by hunters, fly his angry looks,
That I may see him issue conqueror!

ZAB. Now, Mahomet, solicit God himself,
And make him rain down murdering shot from Heaven
To dash the Scythians' brains, and strike them dead,
That dare to manage arms with him
That offered jewels to thy sacred shrine,
When first he warred against the Christians!

[They sound again to the battle within.

ZENO. By this the Turks lie weltering in their blood,
And Tamburlaine is Lord of Africa.

ZAB. Thou art deceived.—I heard the trumpets sound,
As when my emperor overthrew the Greeks,
And led them captive into Africa.
Straight will I use thee as thy pride deserves—
Prepare thyself to live and die my slave.

ZENO. If Mahomet should come from Heaven and swear
My royal lord is slain or conquerèd,
Yet should he not persuade me otherwise
But that he lives and will be conqueror.

Re-enter BAJAZETH, *pursued by* TAMBURLAINE; *they fight, and* BAJAZETH *is overcome.*

TAMB. Now, king of bassoes, who is conqueror?

BAJ. Thou, by the fortune of this damnèd foil.[10]

TAMB. Where are your stout contributory kings?

---

10 Defeat.

Re-enter TECHELLES, THERIDAMAS, *and* USUMCASANE.

TECH. We have their crowns—their bodies strow the field.
TAMB. Each man a crown!—Why kingly fought i' faith.
Deliver them into my treasury.
ZENO. Now let me offer to my gracious lord
His royal crown again so highly won.
TAMB. Nay, take the crown from her, Zenocrate,
And crown me Emperor of Africa.
ZAB. No, Tamburlaine: though now thou gat the best,
Thou shalt not yet be lord of Africa.
THER. Give her the crown, Turkess: you were best.
[*He takes it from her.*
ZAB. Injurious villains!—thieves!—runagates!
How dare you thus abuse my majesty?
THER. Here, madam, you are Empress; she is none.
[*Gives it to* ZENOCRATE.
TAMB. Not now, Theridamas; her time is past.
The pillars that have bolstered up those terms,
Are fallen in clusters at my conquering feet.
ZAB. Though he be prisoner, he may be ransomed.
TAMB. Not all the world shall ransom Bajazeth.
BAJ. Ah, fair Zabina! we have lost the field;
And never had the Turkish emperor
So great a foil by any foreign foe.
Now will the Christian miscreants be glad,
Ringing with joy their superstitious bells,
And making bonfires for my overthrow.
But, ere I die, those foul idolaters
Shall make me bonfires with their filthy bones.
For though the glory of this day be lost,
Afric and Greece have garrisons enough
To make me sovereign of the earth again.
TAMB. Those wallèd garrisons will I subdue,
And write myself great lord of Africa.
So from the East unto the furthest West
Shall Tamburlaine extend his puissant arm.
The galleys and those pilling[11] brigandines,
That yearly sail to the Venetian gulf,
And hover in the Straits for Christians' wreck,
Shall lie at anchor in the isle Asant,

---

11 Plundering.

Until the Persian fleet and men of war,
Sailing along the oriental sea,
Have fetched about the Indian continent,
Even from Persepolis to Mexico,
And thence unto the straits of Jubaltèr;[12]
Where they shall meet and join their force in one
Keeping in awe the bay of Portingale,[13]
And all the ocean by the British shore;
And by this means I'll win the world at last.

BAJ. Yet set a ransom on me, Tamburlaine.

TAMB. What, think'st thou Tamburlaine esteems thy gold?
I'll make the kings of India, ere I die,
Offer their mines to sue for peace to me,
And dig for treasure to appease my wrath.
Come, bind them both, and one lead in the Turk;
The Turkess let my love's maid lead away.

[*They bind them.*

BAJ. Ah, villains!—dare you touch my sacred arms?
O Mahomet!—O sleepy Mahomet!

ZAB. O cursèd Mahomet, that mak'st us thus
The slaves to Scythians rude and barbarous!

TAMB. Come, bring them in; and for this happy conquest,
Triumph and solemnise a martial feast. [*Exeunt.*

---

12 Gibraltar.
13 Biscay.

ACT THE FOURTH.

Scene I.

Enter the Soldan *of* Egypt, Capolin, Lords, *and a* Messenger.

Sold. Awake, ye men of Memphis!—hear the clang
Of Scythian trumpets!—hear the basilisks,[1]
That, roaring, shake Damascus' turrets down!
The rogue of Volga holds Zenocrate,
The Soldan's daughter, for his concubine,
And with a troop of thieves and vagabonds,
Hath spread his colours to our high disgrace,
While you, faint-hearted, base Egyptians,
Lie slumbering on the flowery banks of Nile,
As crocodiles that unaffrighted rest,
While thundering cannons rattle on their skins.
Mes. Nay, mighty Soldan, did your greatness see
The frowning looks of fiery Tamburlaine,
That with his terror and imperious eyes,
Commands the hearts of his associates,
It might amaze your royal majesty.
Sold. Villain, I tell thee, were that Tamburlaine
As monstrous as Gorgon[2] prince of hell,
The Soldan would not start a foot from him.
But speak, what power hath he?
Mes. Mighty lord,
Three hundred thousand men in armour clad,
Upon their prancing steeds disdainfully,
With wanton paces trampling on the ground:
Five hundred thousand footmen threatening shot,

---

1 Pieces of ordnance, so called from their fancied resemblance to the fabulous serpent of that name.
2 *i.e.* Demogorgon.

Shaking their swords, their spears, and iron bills,
Environing their standard round, that stood
As bristle-pointed as a thorny wood:
Their warlike engines and munition
Exceed the forces of their martial men.

SOLD. Nay, could their numbers countervail the stars,
Or ever-drizzling drops of April showers,
Or withered leaves that autumn shaketh down,
Yet would the Soldan by his conquering power
So scatter and consume them in his rage,
That not a man should live to rue their fall.

CAPO. So might your highness, had you time to sort
Your fighting men, and raise your royal host;
But Tamburlaine, by expedition,
Advantage takes of your unreadiness.

SOLD. Let him take all the advantages he can.
Were all the world conspired to fight for him,
Nay, were he devil, as he is no man,
Yet in revenge of fair Zenocrate,
Whom he detaineth in despite of us,
This arm should send him down to Erebus,
To shroud his shame in darkness of the night.

MES. Pleaseth your mightiness to understand,
His resolution far exeedeth all.
The first day when he pitcheth down his tents,
White is their hue, and on his silver crest,
A snowy feather spangled white he bears,
To signify the mildness of his mind,
That, satiate with spoil, refuseth blood.
But when Aurora mounts the second time
As red as scarlet is his furniture;
Then must his kindled wrath be quenched with blood,
Not sparing any that can manage arms;
But if these threats move not submission,
Black are his colours, black pavilion;
His spear, his shield, his horse, his armour, plumes,
And jetty feathers, menace death and hell!
Without respect of sex, degree, or age,
He razeth all his foes with fire and sword.

SOLD. Merciless villain!—peasant, ignorant
Of lawful arms or martial discipline!
Pillage and murder are his usual trades.
The slave usurps the glorious name of war.

See, Capolin, the fair Arabian king,
That hath been disappointed by this slave
Of my fair daughter, and his princely love,
May have fresh warning to go war with us,
And be revenged for her disparagement. [*Exeunt.*

SCENE II

Enter TAMBURLAINE, TECHELLES, THERIDAMAS, USUMCASANE, ZENOCRATE, ANIPPE, *two* Moors *drawing* BAJAZETH *in a cage, and* ZABINA *following him.*

TAMB. Bring out my footstool.
[BAZAJETH *is taken out of the cage.*

BAJ. Ye holy priests of Heavenly Mahomet,
That, sacrificing, slice and cut your flesh,
Staining his altars with your purple blood;
Make Heaven to frown and every fixèd star
To suck up poison from the moorish fens,
And pour it in this glorious[1] tyrant's throat!

TAMB. The chiefest God, first mover of that sphere,
Enchased with thousands ever-shining lamps,
Will sooner burn the glorious frame of Heaven,
Than it should so conspire my overthrow.
But, villain! thou that wishest this to me,
Fall prostrate on the low disdainful earth,
And be the footstool of great Tamburlaine,
That I may rise into my royal throne.

BAJ. First shalt thou rip my bowels with thy sword,
And sacrifice my soul to death and hell,
Before I yield to such a slavery.

TAMB. Base villain, vassal, slave to Tamburlaine!
Unworthy to embrace or touch the ground,
That bears the honour of my royal weight;
Stoop, villain, stoop!—Stoop! for so he bids
That may command thee piecemeal to be torn,
Or scattered like the lofty cedar trees
Strook with the voice of thundering Jupiter.

BAJ. Then, as I look down to the damnèd fiends,

1 Boastful.

Fiends look on me! and thou, dread god of hell,
With ebon sceptre strike this hateful earth,
And make it swallow both of us at once!
[TAMBURLAINE *steps upon him to mount his throne.*

TAMB. Now clear the triple region of the air,
And let the majesty of Heaven behold
Their scourge and terror tread on emperors.
Smile stars, that reigned at my nativity,
And dim the brightness of your neighbour lamps!
Disdain to borrow light of Cynthia!
For I, the chiefest lamp of all the earth,
First rising in the East with mild aspèct,
But fixèd now in the meridian line,
Will send up fire to your turning spheres,
And cause the sun to borrow light of you.
My sword struck fire from his coat of steel,
Even in Bithynia, when I took this Turk;
As when a fiery exhalation,
Wrapt in the bowels of a freezing cloud
Fighting for passage, makes the welkin crack,
And casts a flash of lightning to the earth:
But ere I march to wealthy Persia,
Or leave Damascus and the Egyptian fields,
As was the fame of Clymene's brain-sick son,
That almost brent the axle-tree of Heaven,
So shall our swords, our lances, and our shot
Fill all the air with fiery meteors:
Then when the sky shall wax as red as blood
It shall be said I made it red myself,
To make me think of nought but blood and war.

ZAB. Unworthy king, that by thy cruelty
Unlawfully usurp'st the Persian seat,
Dar'st thou that never saw an emperor,
Before thou met my husband in the field,
Being thy captive, thus abuse his state,
Keeping his kingly body in a cage,
That roofs of gold and sun-bright palaces
Should have prepared to entertain his grace?
And treading him beneath thy loathsome feet,
Whose feet the kings of Africa have kissed.

TECH. You must devise some torment worse, my lord,
To make these captives rein their lavish tongues.

TAMB. Zenocrate, look better to your slave.
ZENO. She is my handmaid's slave, and she shall look
That these abuses flow not from her tongue:
Chide her, Anippe.
ANIP. Let these be warnings for you then, my slave,
How you abuse the person of the king;
Or else I swear to have you whipt, stark-naked.
BAJ. Great Tamburlaine, great in my overthrow,
Ambitious pride shall make thee fall as low,
For treading on the back of Bajazeth,
That should be horsèd on four mighty kings.
TAMB. Thy names, and titles, and thy dignities
Are fled from Bajazeth and remain with me,
That will maintain it 'gainst a world of kings.
Put him in again. [*They put him back into the cage.*
BAJ. Is this a place for mighty Bajazeth?
Confusion light on him that helps thee thus!
TAMB. There, whiles he lives, shall Bajazeth be kept;
And, where I go, be thus in triumph drawn;
And thou, his wife, shall feed him with the scraps
My servitors shall bring thee from my board;
For he that gives him other food than this,
Shall sit by him and starve to death himself;
This is my mind and I will have it so.
Not all the kings and emperors of the earth,
If they would lay their crowns before my feet,
Shall ransom him, or take him from his cage.
The ages that shall talk of Tamburlaine,
Even from this day to Plato's wondrous year,[2]
Shall talk how I have handled Bajazeth;
These Moors, that drew him from Bithynia,
To fair Damascus, where we now remain,
Shall lead him with us wheresoe'er we go.
Techelles, and my loving followers,
Now may we see Damascus' lofty towers,
Like to the shadows of Pyramides
That with their beauties grace the Memphian fields:
The golden statue of their feathered bird
That spreads her wings upon the city's walls
Shall not defend it from our battering shot:

---

2 See Plato's *Timæus.*

The townsmen mask in silk and cloth of gold,
And every house is as a treasury:
The men, the treasure, and the town is ours.

THER. Your tents of white now pitched before the gates,
And gentle flags of amity displayed,
I doubt not but the governor will yield,
Offering Damascus to your majesty.

TAMB. So shall he have his life and all the rest:
But if he stay until the bloody flag
Be once advanced on my vermilion tent,
He dies, and those that kept us out so long.
And when they see us march in black array,
With mournful streamers hanging down their heads,
Were in that city all the world contained,
Not one should 'scape, but perish by our swords.

ZENO. Yet would you have some pity for my sake,
Because it is my country, and my father's.

TAMB. Not for the world, Zenocrate; I've sworn.
Come; bring in the Turk. [*Exeunt.*

SCENE III

Enter the SOLDAN, *the* KING *of* ARABIA, CAPOLIN, *and* Soldiers *with colours flying.*

SOLD. Methinks we march as Meleager did,
Environèd with brave Argolian knights,
To chase the savage Calydonian boar,
Or Cephalus with lusty Theban youths
Against the wolf that angry Themis sent
To waste and spoil the sweet Aonian fields,
A monster of five hundred thousand heads,
Compact of rapine, piracy, and spoil.
The scum of men, the hate and scourge of God,
Raves in Ægyptia, and annoyeth us.
My lord, it is the bloody Tamburlaine,
A sturdy felon and a base-bred thief,
By murder raisèd to the Persian crown,
That dares control us in our territories.
To tame the pride of this presumptuous beast,
Join your Arabians with the Soldan's power,
Let us unite our royal bands in one,
And hasten to remove Damascus' siege.

It is a blemish to the majesty
And high estate of mighty emperors,
That such a base usurping vagabond
Should brave a king, or wear a princely crown.

K. OF ARAB. Renownèd Soldan, have you lately heard
The overthrow of mighty Bajazeth
About the confines of Bithynia?
The slavery wherewith he persecutes
The noble Turk and his great emperess?

SOLD. I have, and sorrow for his bad success;
But noble lord of great Arabia,
Be so persuaded that the Soldan is
No more dismayed with tidings of his fall,
Than in the haven when the pilot stands,
And views a stranger's ship rent in the winds,
And shiverèd against a craggy rock;
Yet in compassion to his wretched state,
A sacred vow to Heaven and him I make,
Confirming it with Ibis' holy name.
That Tamburlaine shall rue the day, the hour,
Wherein he wrought such ignominious wrong
Unto the hallowed person of a prince,
Or kept the fair Zenocrate so long
As concubine, I fear, to feed his lust.

K. OF ARAB. Let grief and fury hasten on revenge;
Let Tamburlaine for his offences feel
Such plagues as we and Heaven can pour on him.
I long to break my spear upon his crest,
And prove the weight of his victorious arm;
For Fame, I fear, hath been too prodigal
In sounding through the world his partial praise.

SOLD. Capolin, hast thou surveyed our powers?

CAPO. Great Emperors of Egypt and Arabia,
The number of your hosts united is
A hundered and fifty thousand horse;
Two hundred thousand foot, brave men-at-arms,
Courageous, and full of hardiness.
As frolic as the hunters in the chase
Of savage beasts amid the desert woods.

K. OF ARAB. My mind presageth fortunate success;
And Tamburlaine, my spirit doth foresee
The utter ruin of thy men and thee.

SOLD. Then rear your standards; let your sounding drums
Direct our soldiers to Damascus' walls.

Now, Tamburlaine, the mighty Soldan comes,
And leads with him the great Arabian king,
To dim thy baseness and obscurity,
Famous for nothing but for theft and spoil;
To raze and scatter thy inglorious crew
Of Scythians and slavish Persians. [*Exeunt.*

SCENE IV.

A *Banquet set out; to it come* TAMBURLAINE, *all in scarlet* ZENOCRATE, THERIDAMAS, TECHELLES, USUMCASANE, BAJAZETH *in his cage*, ZABINA, *and others.*

TAMB. Now hang our bloody colours by Damascus,
Reflexing hues of blood upon their heads,
While they walk quivering on their city walls,
Half dead for fear before they feel my wrath,
Then let us freely banquet and carouse
Full bowls of wine unto the god of war
That means to fill your helmets full of gold,
And make Damascus spoils as rich to you,
As was to Jason Colchos' golden fleece.—
And now, Bajazeth, hast thou any stomach?
BAJ. Ay, such a stomach, cruel Tamburlaine, as I
could willingly feed upon thy blood-raw heart.
TAMB. Nay, thine own is easier to come by; pluck
out that: and 'twill serve thee and thy wife:
Well, Zenocrate, Techelles, and the rest,
fall to your victuals.
BAJ. Fall to, and never may your meat digest!
Ye Furies, that can mask invisible,
Dive to the bottom of Avernus' pool,
And in your hands bring hellish poison up
And squeeze it in the cup of Tamburlaine!
Or, wingèd snakes of Lerna, cast your stings,
And leave your venoms in this tyrant's dish!
ZAB. And may this banquet prove as ominous
As Progne's[1] to the adulterous Thracian king,
That fed upon the substance of his child.

1 *i.e.* Procne.

ZENO. My lord, how can you suffer these
Outrageous curses by these slaves of yours?

TAMB. To let them see, divine Zenocrate,
I glory in the curses of my foes,
Having the power from the imperial Heaven
To turn them all upon their proper heads.

TECH. I pray you give them leave, madam; this speech is a goodly refreshing to them.

THER. But if his highness would let them be fed, it would do them more good.

TAMB. Sirrah, why fall you not to?—are you so daintily brought up, you cannot eat your own flesh?

BAJ. First, legions of devils shall tear thee in pieces.

USUM. Villain, know'st thou to whom thou speakest?

TAMB. O, let him alone. Here; eat, sir; take it from my sword's point, or I'll thrust it to thy heart.

[BAJAZETH *takes it and stamps upon it.*

THER. He stamps it under his feet, my lord.

TAMB. Take it up, villain, and eat it; or I will make thee slice the brawns of thy arms into carbonadoes[2] and eat them.

USUM. Nay, 'twere better he killed his wife, and then she shall be sure not to be starved, and he be provided for a month's victual beforehand.

TAMB. Here is my dagger: dispatch her while she is fat, for if she live but a while longer, she will fall into a consumption with fretting, and then she will not be worth the eating.

THER. Dost thou think that Mahomet will suffer this?

TECH. 'Tis like he will when he cannot let[3] it.

TAMB. Go to; fall to your meat.—What, not a bit! Belike he hath not been watered to-day; give him some drink.

[*They give* BAJAZETH *water to drink, and he flings it upon the ground.*

TAMB. Fast, and welcome, sir, while[4] hunger make you eat. How now, Zenocrate, do not the Turk and his wife make a goodly show at a banquet?

ZENO. Yes, my lord.

THER. Methinks, 'tis a great deal better than a consort[5] of music.

TAMB. Yet music would do well to cheer up Zenocrate. Pray thee, tell, why thou art so sad?—If thou wilt have a song, the Turk shall strain his voice. But why is it?

---

2 Rashers.
3 Hinder.
4 Until.
5 Band.

ZENO. My lord, to see my father's town besieged,
The country wasted where myself was born,
How can it but afflict my very soul?
If any love remain in you, my lord,
Or if my love unto your majesty
May merit favour at your highness' hands,
Then raise your siege from fair Damascus' walls,
And with my father take a friendly truce.
TAMB. Zenocrate, were Egypt Jove's own land,
Yet would I with my sword make Jove to stoop.
I will confute those blind geographers
That make a triple region in the world,
Excluding regions which I mean to trace,
And with this pen[6] reduce them to a map,
Calling the provinces cities and towns,
After my name and thine, Zenocrate.
Here at Damascus will I make the point
That shall begin the perpendicular;
And would'st thou have me buy thy father's love
With such a loss?—Tell me, Zenocrate.
ZENO. Honour still wait on happy Tamburlaine;
Yet give me leave to plead for him my lord.
TAMB. Content thyself: his person shall be safe
And all the friends of fair Zenocrate,
If with their lives they may be pleased to yield,
Or may be forced to make me Emperor;
For Egypt and Arabia must be mine.—
Feed, you slave; thou may'st think thyself happy to be fed from my trencher.
BAJ. My empty stomach, full of idle heat,
Draws bloody humours from my feeble parts,
Preserving life by hasting cruel death.
My veins are pale; my sinews hard and dry;
My joints benumbed; unless I eat, I die.
ZAB. Eat, Bajazeth: and let us live
In spite of them,—looking some happy power
Will pity and enlarge us.
TAMB. Here, Turk; wilt thou have a clean trencher?
BAJ. Ay, tyrant, and more meat.
TAMB. Soft, sir; you must be dieted; too much eating will make you surfeit.

6 Meaning his sword.

THER. So it would, my lord, 'specially having so small a walk and so little exercise.

[*A second course of crowns is brought in.*

TAMB. Theridamas, Techelles and Casane, her are the cates you desire to finger, are they not?

THER. Ay, my lord: but none save kings must feed with these.

TECH. 'Tis enough for us to see them, and for Tamburlaine only to enjoy them.

TAMB. Well; here is now to the Soldan of Egypt, the King of Arabia, and the Governor of Damascus. Now take these three crowns, and pledge me, my contributory kings.—I crown you here, Theridamas, King of Argier; Techelles, King of Fez; and Usumcasane, King of Moroccus. How say you to this, Turk? These are not your contributory kings.

BAJ. Nor shall they long be thine, I warrant them.

TAMB. Kings of Argier, Moroccus, and of Fez,
You that have marched with happy Tamburlaine
As far as from the frozen plage[7] of Heaven,
Unto the watery morning's ruddy bower,
And thence by land unto the torrid zone,
Deserve these titles I endow you with,
By valour and by magnanimity.
Your births shall be no blemish to your fame,
For virtue is the fount whence honour springs,
And they are worthy she investeth kings.

THER. And since your highness hath so well vouchsafed;
If we deserve them not with higher meeds
Than erst our states and actions have retained
Take them away again and make us slaves.

TAMB. Well said, Theridamas; when holy fates
Shall 'stablish me in strong Ægyptia,
We mean to travel to the antarctic pole,
Conquering the people underneath our feet,
And be renowned as never emperors were.
Zenocrate, I will not crown thee yet,
Until with greater honours I be graced. [*Exeunt.*

7 Shore: Fr. *plage.*

ACT THE FIFTH.

SCENE I.

Enter the GOVERNOR *of* DAMASCUS, *with several* Citizens, *and four* Virgins, *having branches of laurel in their hands.*

GOV. Still doth this man, or rather god of war,
Batter our walls and beat our turrets down;
And to resist with longer stubbornness
Or hope of rescue from the Soldan's power,
Were but to bring our wilful overthrow,
And make us desperate of our threatened lives.
We see his tents have now been altered
With terrors to the last and cruellest hue.
His coal-black colours everywhere advanced,
Threaten our city with a general spoil;
And if we should with common rites of arms
Offer our safeties to his clemency,
I fear the custom, proper to his sword,
Which he observes as parcel of his fame,
Intending so to terrify the world,
By any innovation or remorse
Will never be dispensed with till our deaths;
Therefore, for these our harmless virgins' sakes,
Whose honours and whose lives rely on him,
Let us have hope that their unspotted prayers,
Their blubbered[1] cheeks, and hearty, humble moans,
Will melt his fury into some remorse,[2]
And use us like a loving conqueror.

1ST VIRG. If humble suits or imprecations,[3]

---

1 The word formerly conveyed no kind of ludicrous impression.
2 Pity.
3 Prayers.

(Uttered with tears of wretchedness and blood
Shed from the heads and hearts of all our sex,
Some made your wives and some your children)
Might have entreated your obdurate breasts
To entertain some care of our securities
Whiles only danger beat upon our walls.
These more than dangerous warrants of our death
Had never been erected as they be,
Nor you depend on such weak helps as we.

GOV. Well, lovely virgins, think our country's care,
Our love of honour, loath to be inthralled
To foreign powers and rough imperious yokes,
Would not with too much cowardice or fear,
(Before all hope of rescue were denied)
Submit yourselves and us to servitude.
Therefore in that your safeties and our own,
Your honours, liberties, and lives were weighed
In equal care and balance with our own,
Endure as we the malice of our stars,
The wrath of Tamburlaine and power of wars;
Or be the means the overweighing heavens
Have kept to qualify these hot extremes,
And bring us pardon in your cheerful looks.

2ND VIRG. Then here before the majesty of heaven
And holy patrons of Ægyptia,
With knees and hearts submissive we entreat
Grace to our words and pity to our looks
That this device may prove propitious,
And through the eyes and ears of Tamburlaine
Convey events of mercy to his heart;
Grant that these signs of victory we yield
May bind the temples of his conquering head,
To hide the folded furrows of his brows,
And shadow his displeasèd countenance
With happy looks of ruth and lenity.
Leave us, my lord, and loving countrymen;
What simple virgins may persuade, we will.

GOV. Farewell, sweet virgins, on whose safe return
Depends our city, liberty, and lives.

[*Exeunt* GOVERNOR *and* CITIZENS; *the* Virgins *remain.*

Enter TAMBURLAINE, *all in black and very melancholy,* TECHELLES, THERIDAMAS, USUMCASANE, *with others.*

TAMB. What, are the turtles frayed out of their nests?
Alas, poor fools! must you be first shall feel
The sworn destruction of Damascus?
They knew my custom; could they not as well
Have sent ye out, when first my milk-white flags,
Through which sweet Mercy threw her gentle beams,
Reflexing them on your disdainful eyes,
As now, when fury and incensèd hate
Flings slaughtering terror from my coal-black tents,
And tells for truth submission comes too late?

1ST VIRG. Most happy King and Emperor of the earth,
Image of honour and nobility,
For whom the powers divine have made the world,
And on whose throne the holy Graces sit;
In whose sweet person is comprised the sum
Of Nature's skill and Heavenly majesty;
Pity our plights! O pity poor Damascus!
Pity old age, within whose silver hairs
Honour and reverence evermore have reigned!
Pity the marriage bed, where many a lord,
In prime and glory of his loving joy,
Embraceth now with tears of ruth and blood
The jealous body of his fearful wife,
Whose cheeks and hearts so punished with conceit,
To think thy puissant never-stayèd arm,
Will part their bodies, and prevent their souls
From heavens of comfort yet their age might bear,
Now wax all pale and withered to the death,
As well for grief our ruthless governor
Hath thus refused the mercy of thy hand,
(Whose sceptre angels kiss and furies dread),
As for their liberties, their loves, or lives!
O then for these, and such as we ourselves,
For us, our infants, and for all our bloods,
That never nourished thought against thy rule,
Pity, O pity, sacred Emperor,
The prostrate service of this wretched town,
And take in sign thereof this gilded wreath;
Whereto each man of rule hath given his hand,
And wished, as worthy subjects, happy means
To be investors of thy royal brows
Even with the true Egyptian diadem!

TAMB. Virgins, in vain you labour to prevent

That which mine honour swears shall be performed.
Behold my sword! what see you at the point?
1ST VIRG. Nothing but fear, and fatal steel, my lord.
Tamb. Your fearful minds are thick and misty then;
For there sits Death; there sits imperious Death
Keeping his circuit by the slicing edge.
But I am pleased you shall not see him there;
He now is seated on my horsemen's spears,
And on their points his fleshless body feeds.
Techelles, straight go charge a few of them
To charge these dames, and show my servant, Death,
Sitting in scarlet on their armèd spears.
VIRGINS. O pity us!
TAMB. Away with them, I say, and show them Death.
[*The* Virgins *are taken out.*
I will not spare these proud Egyptians,
Nor change my martial observations
For all the wealth of Gihon's golden waves,
Or for the love of Venus, would she leave
The angry god of arms and lie with me.
They have refused the offer of their lives,
And know my customs are as peremptory
As wrathful planets, death, or destiny.

Re-enter TECHELLES.

What, have your horsemen shown the virgins Death?
TECH. They have, my lord, and on Damascus' walls
Have hoisted up their slaughtered carcases.
TAMB. A sight as baneful to their souls, I think,
As are Thessalian drugs or mithridate:[4]
But go, my lords, put the rest to the sword.
[*Exeunt all except* TAMBURLAINE.
Ah, fair Zenocrate!—Divine Zenocrate!—
Fair is too foul an epithet for thee,
That in thy passion[5] for thy country's love,
And fear to see thy kingly father's harm,
With hair dishevelled wip'st thy watery cheeks;
And, like to Flora in her morning pride,
Shaking her silver tresses in the air,
Rain'st on the earth resolvèd pearl in showers,

4 An antidote distilled from poisons.
5 Sorrow.

And sprinklest sapphires on thy shining face,
Where Beauty, mother to the Muses, sits,
And comments volumes with her ivory pen,
Taking instructions from thy flowing eyes;
Eyes that, when Ebena steps to Heaven,
In silence of thy solemn evening's walk,
Make, in the mantle of the richest night,
The moon, the planets, and the meteors, light;
There angels in their crystal armours fight
A doubtful battle with my tempted thoughts
For Egypt's freedom, and the Soldan's life;
His life that so consumes Zenocrate,
Whose sorrows lay more siege unto my soul,
Than all my army to Damascus' walls:
And neither Persia's sovereign, nor the Turk
Troubled my senses with conceit of foil
So much by much as doth Zenocrate.
What is beauty, saith my sufferings, then?
If all the pens that ever poets held
Had fed the feeling of their masters' thoughts,
And every sweetness that inspired their hearts,
Their minds, and muses on admirèd themes;
If all the Heavenly quintessence they still[6]
From their immortal flowers of poesy,
Wherein, as in a mirror, we perceive
The highest reaches of a human wit;
If these had made one poem's period,
And all combined in beauty's worthiness,
Yet should there hover in their restless heads
One thought, one grace, one wonder, at the least,
Which into words no virtue can digest.
But how unseemly is it for my sex,
My discipline of arms and chivalry,
My nature, and the terror of my name,
To harbour thoughts effeminate and faint!
Save only that in beauty's just applause,
With whose instinct the soul of man is touched;
And every warrior that is wrapt with love
Of fame, of valour, and of victory,
Must needs have beauty beat on his conceits:
I thus conceiving and subduing both

6 *i.e.*, Distil.

That which hath stooped the chiefest of the gods,
Even from the fiery-spangled veil of Heaven,
To feel the lovely warmth of shepherds' flames,
And mask in cottages of strowèd reeds,
Shall give the world to note for all my birth,
That virtue solely is the sum of glory,
And fashions men with true nobility.—
Who's within there?

Enter Attendants.

Hath Bajazeth been fed to-day?
ATTEN. Ay, my lord.
TAMB. Bring him forth; and let us know if the town be ransacked.
[*Exeunt* Attendants.

Enter TECHELLES, THERIDAMAS, USUMCASANE, *and others.*

TECH. The town is ours, my lord, and fresh supply
Of conquest and of spoil is offered us.
TAMB. That's well, Techelles; what's the news?
TECH. The Soldan and the Arabian king together,
March on us with such eager violence,
As if there were no way but one with us.[7]
TAMB. No more there is not, I warrant thee, Techelles.

Attendants *bring in* BAZAJETH *in his cage, followed by* ZABINA; *then exeunt.*

THER. We know the victory is ours, my lord;
But let us save the reverend Soldan's life,
For fair Zenocrate that so laments his state.
TAMB. That will we chiefly see unto, Theridamas,
For sweet Zenocrate, whose worthiness
Deserves a conquest over every heart.
And now, my footstool, if I lose the field,
You hope of liberty and restitution?
Here let him stay, my masters, from the tents,
Till we have made us ready for the field.
Pray for us, Bajazeth; we are going.
[*Exeunt* TAMBURLAINE, TECHELLES, USUMCASANE, *and* Persians.
BAJ. Go, never to return with victory.
Millions of men encompass thee about,
And gore thy body with as many wounds!

---

7 *i.e.* As if we must lose our lives.

Sharp, forkèd arrows light upon thy horse!
Furies from the black Cocytus lake,
Break up the earth, and with their firebrands
Enforce thee run upon the baneful pikes!
Volleys of shot pierce through thy charmèd skin,
And every bullet dipt in poisoned drugs!
Or, roaring cannons sever all thy joints,
Making thee mount as high as eagles soar!
ZAB. Let all the swords and lances in the field
Stick in his breast as in their proper rooms!
At every pore let blood come dropping forth,
That lingering pains may massacre his heart,
And madness send his damnèd soul to hell!
BAJ. Ah, fair Zabina! we may curse his power;
The heavens may frown, the earth for anger quake:
But such a star hath influence on his sword,
As rules the skies and countermands the gods
More than Cimmerian Styx or destiny;
And then shall we in this detested guise,
With shame, with hunger, and with horror stay,
Griping our bowels with retorquèd[8] thoughts
And have no hope to end our ecstasies.
ZAB. Then is there left no Mahomet, no God,
No fiend, no fortune, nor no hope of end
To our infàmous, monstrous slaveries.
Gape earth, and let the fiends infernal view
A hell as hopeless and as full of fear
As are the blasted banks of Erebus,
Where shaking ghosts with ever howling groans
Hover about the ugly ferryman,
To get a passage to Elysium!
Why should we live? O wretches, beggars, slaves!
Why live we, Bajazeth, and build up nests
So high within the region of the air,
By living long in this oppression,
That all the world will see and laugh to scorn
The former triumphs of our mightiness
In this obscure infernal servitude?
BAJ. O life, more loathsome to my vexèd thoughts
Than noisome parbreak[9] of the Stygian snakes,

8 Bent back.
9 Vomit.

Which fills the nooks of hell with standing air,
Infecting all the ghosts with cureless griefs!
O dreary engines of my loathèd sight,
That see my crown, my honour, and my name
Thrust under yoke and thraldom of a thief,
Why feed ye still on day's accursèd beams
And sink not quite into my tortured soul?
You see my wife, my queen, and emperess,
Brought up and proppèd by the hand of fame,
Queen of fifteen contributory queens,
Now thrown to rooms of black abjection,
Smearèd with blots of basest drudgery,
And villainess[10] to shame, disdain, and misery.
Accursèd Bajazeth, whose words of ruth,
(That would with pity cheer Zabina's heart,
And make our souls resolve[11] in ceaseless tears);
Sharp hunger bites upon, and gripes the root,
From whence the issues of my thoughts do break;
O poor Zabina! O my queen! my queen!
Fetch me some water for my burning breast,
To cool and comfort me with longer date,
That in the shortened sequel of my life
I may pour forth my soul into thine arms
With words of love, whose moaning intercourse
Hath hitherto been stayed with wrath and hate
Of our expressless banned inflictions.

ZAB. Sweet Bajazeth, I will prolong thy life,
As long as any blood or spark of breath
Can quench or cool the torments of my grief. [*Exit.*

BAJ. Now, Bajazeth, abridge thy baneful days,
And beat the brains out of thy conquered head,
Since other means are all forbidden me,
That may be ministers of my decay.
O, highest lamp of ever-living Jove,
Accursèd day! infected with my griefs,
Hide now thy stainèd face in endless night,
And shut the windows of the lightsome heavens!
Let ugly Darkness with her rusty coach;
Engirt with tempests, wrapt in pitchy clouds,
Smother the earth with never-fading mists!
And let her horses from their nostrils breathe

10 Slave.
11 Dissolve.

Rebellious winds and dreadful thunder-claps!
That in this terror Tamburlaine may live,
And my pined soul, resolved in liquid air,
May still excruciate his tormented thoughts!
Then let the stony dart of senseless cold
Pierce through the centre of my withered heart,
And make a passage for my loathèd life!
[*He brains himself against the cage.*

Re-enter ZABINA.

ZAB. What do mine eyes behold? my husband dead
His skull all riven in twain! his brains dashed out,—
The brains of Bajazeth, my lord and sovereign:
O Bajazeth, my husband and my lord!
O Bajazeth! O Turk! O Emperor!
Give him his liquor? not I. Bring milk and fire, and my blood I bring him again.—Tear me in pieces—give me the sword with a ball of wild-fire upon it.—Down with him! Down with him!—Go to my child! Away! Away!—Away! Ah, save that infant! save him, save him!—I, even I, speak to her. The sun was down—streamers white, red, black—here, here, here! Fling the meat in his face—Tamburlaine!—Tamburlaine!—Let the soldiers be buried.—Hell! Death, Tamburlaine, Hell! Make ready my coach, my chair, my jewels.—I come! I come! I come!
[*She runs against the cage and brains herself.*

Enter ZENOCRATE *with* ANIPPE.

ZENO. Wretched Zenocrate!, that liv'st to see
Damascus' walls dyed with Egyptians' blood,
Thy father's subjects and thy countrymen;
The streets strowed with dissevered joints of men
And wounded bodies gasping yet for life:
But most accurst, to see the sun-bright troop
Of heavenly virgins and unspotted maids,
(Whose looks might make the angry god of arms
To break his sword and mildly treat of love),
On horsemen's lances to be hoisted up
And guiltlessly endure a cruel death:
For every fell and stout Tartarian steed,
That stampt on others with their thundering hoofs,
When all their riders charged their quivering spears,
Began to check the ground and rein themselves,
Gazing upon the beauty of their looks.—

Ah Tamburlaine! wert thou the cause of this
That term'st Zenocrate thy dearest love?
Whose lives were dearer to Zenocrate
Than her own life, or aught save thine own love.
But see another bloody spectacle!
Ah, wretched eyes, the enemies of my heart,
How are ye glutted with these grievous objects,
And tell my soul more tales of bleeding ruth!
See, see, Anippe, if they breathe or no.

ANIPPE. No breath, nor sense, nor motion in them both;
Ah, madam! this their slavery hath enforced,
And ruthless cruelty of Tamburlaine.

ZENO. Earth, cast up fountains from thy entrails,
And wet thy cheeks for their untimely deaths!
Shake with their weight in sign of fear and grief!
Blush, Heaven, that gave them honour at their birth
And let them die a death so barbarous!
Those that are proud of fickle empery
And place their chiefest good in earthly pomp,
Behold the Turk and his great Emperess!
Ah, Tamburlaine! my love! sweet Tamburlaine!
That fight'st for sceptres and for slippery crowns,
Behold the Turk and his great Emperess!
Thou, that in conduct of thy happy stars
Sleep'st every night with conquests on thy brows,
And yet would'st shun the wavering turns of war,
In fear and feeling of the like distress
Behold the Turk and his great Emperess!
Ah, mighty Jove and holy Mahomet,
Pardon my love!—O, pardon his contempt
Of earthly fortune and respect of pity,
And let not conquest, ruthlessly pursued,
Be equally against his life incensed
In this great Turk and hapless Emperess!
And pardon me that was not moved with ruth
To see them live so long in misery!
Ah, what may chance to thee, Zenocrate?

ANIPPE. Madam, content yourself, and be resolved
Your love hath Fortune so at his command,
That she shall stay and turn her wheel no more,
As long as life maintains his mighty arm
That fights for honour to adorn your head.

Enter PHILEMUS, *a* Messenger.

ZENO. What other heavy news now brings Philemus?
PHIL. Madam, your father, and the Arabian king,
The first affecter of your excellence,
Comes now, as Turnus 'gainst Æneas did,
Armèd with lance into the Egyptian fields,
Ready for battle 'gainst my lord, the king.
ZENO. Now shame and duty, love and fear present
A thousand sorrows to my martyred soul.
Whom should I wish the fatal victory
When my poor pleasures are divided thus
And racked by duty from my cursèd heart?
My father and my first-betrothèd love
Must fight against my life and present love;
Wherein the change I use condemns my faith,
And makes my deeds infàmous through the world:
But as the gods, to end the Trojans' toil
Prevented Turnus of Lavinia
And fatally enriched Æneas' love,
So for a final issue to my griefs,
To pacify my country and my love
Must Tamburlaine by their resistless pow'rs,
With virtue of a gentle victory
Conclude a league of honour to my hope;
Then, as the Powers divine have pre-ordained,
With happy safety of my father's life
Send like defence of fair Arabia.
[*Trumpets sound to the battle within: afterwards, the* KING *of* ARABIA *enters wounded.*
K. OF ARAB. What cursèd power guides the murdering hands
Of this infàmous tyrant's soldiers.
That no escape may save their enemies,
Nor fortune keep themselves from victory?
Lie down, Arabia, wounded to the death,
And let Zenocrate's fair eyes behold
That, as for her thou bear'st these wretched arms,
Even so for her thou diest in these arms,
Leaving thy blood for witness of thy love.
ZENO. Too dear a witness for such love, my lord,
Behold Zenocrate! the cursèd object,
Whose fortunes never masterèd her griefs;
Behold her wounded, in conceit, for thee,
As much as thy fair body is for me.
K. OF ARAB. Then shall I die with full, contented heart,

Having beheld divine Zenocrate,
Whose sight with joy would take away my life
As now it bringeth sweetness to my wound,
If I had not been wounded as I am.
Ah! that the deadly pangs I suffer now,
Would lend an hour's licence to my tongue,
To make discourse of some sweet accidents
Have chanced thy merits in this worthless bondage;
And that I might be privy to the state
Of thy deserved contentment, and thy love;
But, making now a virtue of thy sight,
To drive all sorrow from my fainting soul,
Since death denies me farther cause of joy,
Deprived of care, my heart with comfort dies,
Since thy desirèd hand shall close mine eyes. [*He dies.*

Re-enter TAMBURLAINE, *leading the* SOLDAN, TECHELLES, THERIDAMAS, USUMCASANE, *with others.*

TAMB. Come, happy father of Zenocrate,
A title higher than thy Soldan's name.
Though my right hand have thus enthrallèd thee,
Thy princely daughter here shall set thee free;
She that hath calmed the fury of my sword,
Which had ere this been bathed in streams of blood
As vast and deep as Euphrates or Nile.
ZENO. O sight thrice welcome to my joyful soul,
To see the king, my father, issue safe
From dangerous battle of my conquering love!
SOLD. Well met, my only dear Zenocrate,
Though with the loss of Egypt and my crown.
TAMB. 'Twas I, my lord, that got the victory,
And therefore grieve not at your overthrow,
Since I shall render all into your hands,
And add more strength to your dominions
Than ever yet confirmed the Egyptian crown.
The god of war resigns his room to me,
Meaning to make me general of the world:
Jove, viewing me in arms, looks pale and wan,
Fearing my power should pull him from his throne.
Where'er I come the Fatal Sisters sweat,
And grisly Death, by running to and fro,
To do their ceaseless homage to my sword;
And here in Afric, where it seldom rains,

Since I arrived with my triumphant host,
Have swelling clouds, drawn from wide-gasping wounds,
Been oft resolved in bloody purple showers,
A meteor that might terrify the earth,
And make it quake at every drop it drinks.
Millions of souls sit on the banks of Styx
Waiting the back return of Charon's boat;
Hell and Elysium swarm with ghosts of men,
That I have sent from sundry foughten fields,
To spread my fame through hell and up to Heaven.
And see, my lord, a sight of strange import,
Emperors and kings lie breathless at my feet:
The Turk and his great Empress, as it seems,
Left to themselves while we were at the fight,
Have desperately dispatched their slavish lives:
With them Arabia, too, hath left his life:
All sights of power to grace my victory;
And such are objects fit for Tamburlaine;
Wherein, as in a mirror, may be seen
His honour, that consists in shedding blood,
When men presume to manage arms with him.

SOLD. Mighty hath God and Mahomet made thy hand,
Renownèd Tamburlaine! to whom all kings
Of force must yield their crowns and emperies;
And I am pleased with this my overthrow,
If, as beseems a person of thy state,
Thou hast with honour used Zenocrate.

TAMB. Her state and person want no pomp, you see;
And for all blot of foul inchastity
I record Heaven her heavenly self is clear:
Then let me find no farther time to grace
Her princely temples with the Persian crown.
But here these kings that on my fortunes wait,
And have been crowned for provèd worthiness,
Even by this hand that shall establish them,
Shall now, adjoining all their hands with mine,
Invest her here the Queen of Persia.
What saith the noble Soldan and Zenocrate!

SOLD. I yield with thanks and protestations
Of endless honour to thee for her love.

TAMB. Then doubt I not but fair Zenocrate
Will soon consent to satisfy us both.

ZENO. Else should I much forget myself, my lord.

THER. Then let us set the crown upon her head,
That long hath lingered for so high a seat.
TECH. My hand is ready to perform the deed;
For now her marriage-time shall work us rest.
USUM. And here's the crown, my lord; help set it on.
TAMB. Then sit thou down, divine Zenocrate;
And here we crown thee Queen of Persia,
And all the kingdoms and dominions
That late the power of Tamburlaine subdued.
As Juno, when the giants were suppressed,
That darted mountains at her brother Jove,
So looks my love, shadowing in her brows
Triumphs and trophies for my victories;
Or, as Latona's daughter, bent to arms,
Adding more courage to my conquering mind.
To gratify the sweet Zenocrate,
Egyptians, Moors, and men of Asia,
From Barbary unto the western India,
Shall pay a yearly tribute to thy sire:
And from the bounds of Afric to the banks
Of Ganges shall his mighty arm extend.
And now, my lords and loving followers,
That purchased kingdoms by your martial deeds,
Cast off your armour, put on scarlet robes,
Mount up your royal places of estate,
Environèd with troops of noblemen,
And there make laws to rule your provinces.
Hang up your weapons on Alcides' post,
For Tamburlaine takes truce with all the world.
Thy first-betrothèd love, Arabia,
Shall we with honour, as beseems, entomb
With this great Turk and his fair Emperess.
Then, after all these solemn exequies,
We will our rites of marriage solemnise.

Tamburlaine

PART THE SECOND

The Prologue

The general welcomes Tamburlaine received,
When he arrivèd last upon the stage,
Hath made our poet pen his Second Part,
Where death cuts off the progress of his pomp,
And murderous fates throw all his triumphs down.
But what became of fair Zenocrate,
And with how many cities' sacrifice
He celebrated her sad funeral,
Himself in presence shall unfold at large.

Dramatis Personæ

TAMBURLAINE, King of Persia.
CALYPHAS, AMYRAS, CELEBINUS, His sons.
TECHELLES, King of Fez.
THERIDAMAS, King of Argier.
USUMCASANE, King of Morocco.
ORCANES, King of Natolia.
KING of JERUSALEM.
KING of TREBIZOND.
KING of SORIA.
KING of AMASIA.
GAZELLUS, Viceroy of Byron.
URIBASSA.
SIGISMUND, King of Hungary.
FREDERICK, BALDWIN, Lords of Buda and Bohemia.
CALLAPINE, son to BAJAZETH.
ALMEDA, his Keeper.
PERDICAS, Servant to CALYPHAS.
GOVERNOR of BABYLON.
MAXIMUS.
CAPTAIN of BALSERA.
His Son.
Physicians.
Another Captain.
Lords, Citizens, Soldiers, &c.

ZENOCRATE, Wife of TAMBURLAINE.
OLYMPIA, Wife of the Captain of Balsera.
Turkish Concubines.

No list of the characters is given in the early editions; the omission is frequent in plays of this period.

ACT THE FIRST.

SCENE I.

Enter ORCANES, King *of* Natolia, GAZELLUS, Viceroy *of* Byron, URIBASSA, *and their* Train, *with drums and trumpets.*

ORC. Egregious viceroys of these eastern parts,
Placed by the issue of great Bajazeth,
And sacred lord, the mighty Callapine,
Who lives in Egypt, prisoner to that slave
Which kept his father in an iron cage;—
Now have we marched from fair Natolia
Two hundred leagues, and on Danubius' banks
Our warlike host, in complete armour, rest,
Where Sigismund, the king of Hungary,
Should meet our person to conclude a truce.
What! shall we parley with the Christian?
Or cross the stream, and meet him in the field?

GAZ. King of Natolia, let us treat of peace;
We are all glutted with the Christians' blood,
And have a greater foe to fight against,—
Proud Tamburlaine, that, now in Asia,
Near Guyron's head doth set his conq'ring feet,
And means to fire Turkey as he goes.
'Gainst him, my lord, you must address your power.

URI. Besides, King Sigismund hath brought from Christendom,
More than his camp of stout Hungarians,—
Sclavonians, Almain rutters,[1] Muffes, and Danes.
That with the halberd, lance, and murdering axe,
Will hazard that we might with surety hold.

ORC. Though from the shortest northern parallel,
Vast Grantland[2] compassed with the Frozen Sea,

1 Troopers: Germ. *Reiter*.
2 Greenland.

(Inhabited with tall and sturdy men,
Giants as big as hugy Polypheme),
Millions of soldiers cut the arctic line,
Bringing the strength of Europe to these arms,
Our Turkey blades shall glide through all their throats,
And make this champion[3] mead a bloody fen.
Danubius' stream, that runs to Trebizon,
Shall carry, wrapt within his scarlet waves,
As martial presents to our friends at home,
The slaughtered bodies of these Christians.
The Terrene Main, wherein Danubius falls,
Shall, by this battle, be the Bloody Sea.
The wandering sailors of proud Italy
Shall meet those Christians, fleeting with the tide,
Beating in heaps against their argosies,
And make fair Europe, mounted on her bull,
Trapped with the wealth and riches of the world,
Alight, and wear a woful mourning weed.

GAZ. Yet, stout Orcanes, Prorex of the world,
Since Tamburlaine hath mustered all his men,
Marching from Cairo northward with his camp,
To Alexandria, and the frontier towns,
Meaning to make a conquest of our land,
'Tis requisite to parley for a peace
With Sigismund the King of Hungary,
And save our forces for the hot assaults
Proud Tamburlaine intends Natolia.

ORC. Viceroy of Byron, wisely hast thou said.
My realm, the centre of our empery,
Once lost, all Turkey would be overthrown,
And for that cause the Christians shall have peace.
Sclavonians, Almain rutters, Muffes, and Danes,
Fear[4] not Orcanes, but great Tamburlaine;
Nor he, but fortune that hath made him great.
We have revolted Grecians, Albanese,
Sicilians, Jews, Arabians, Turks, and Moors,
Natolians, Syrians, black Egyptians,
Illyrians, Thracians, and Bithynians,
Enough to swallow forceless Sigismund,
Yet scarce enough to encounter Tamburlaine.

---

3 Champaign.
4 *i.e.*, Frighten.

He brings a world of people to the field,
From Scythia to the oriental plage
Of India, where raging Lantchidol[5]
Beats on the regions with his boisterous blows,
That never seaman yet discoverèd.
All Asia is in arms with Tamburlaine,
Even from the midst of fiery Cancer's tropic,
To Amazonia under Capricorn;
And thence as far as Archipelago,
All Afric is in arms with Tamburlaine;
Therefore, viceroy, the Christians must have peace.

Enter SIGISMUND, FREDERICK, BALDWIN, *and their* Train, *with drums and trumpets.*

SIG. Orcanes, (as our legates promised thee),
We, with our peers, have crossed Danubius' stream
To treat of friendly peace or deadly war.
Take which thou wilt, for as the Romans used,
I here present thee with a naked sword;
Wilt thou have war, then shake this blade at me;
If peace, restore it to my hands again,
And I will sheath it, to confirm the same.
ORC. Stay, Sigismund! forget'st thou I am he
That with the cannon shook Vienna walls,
And made it dance upon the continent,
As when the massy substance of the earth
Quiver about the axle-tree of Heaven?
Forget'st thou that I sent a shower of darts,
Mingled with powdered shot and feathered steel,
So thick upon the blink-eyed burghers' heads,
That thou thyself, then county palatine,
The King of Boheme, and the Austric Duke,
Sent heralds out, which basely on their knees
In all your names desired a truce of me?
Forget'st thou, that to have me raise my siege,
Waggons of gold were set before my tents,
Stampt with the princely fowl, that in her wings,
Carries the fearful thunderbolts of Jove?
How canst thou think of this, and offer war?

5 Lantchidol is that part of the Indian Ocean which lies between Java and New Holland.

SIG. Vienna was besieged, and I was there,
Then county palatine, but now a king,
And what we did was in extremity.
But now, Orcanes, view my royal host,
That hides these plains, and seems as vast and wide,
As doth the desert of Arabia
To those that stand on Bagdet's lofty tower;
Or as the ocean, to the traveller
That rests upon the snowy Apennines;
And tell me whether I should stoop so low,
Or treat of peace with the Natolian king.
GAZ. Kings of Natolia and of Hungary,
We came from Turkey to confirm a league,
And not to dare each other to the field.
A friendly parley might become you both.
FRED. And we from Europe, to the same intent,
Which if your general refuse or scorn,
Our tents are pitched, our men stand in array,
Ready to charge you ere you stir your feet.
ORC. So prest[6] are we; but yet, if Sigismund
Speak as a friend, and stand not upon terms,
Here is his sword,—let peace be ratified
On these conditions, specified before,
Drawn with advice of our ambassadors.
SIG. Then here I sheathe it, and give thee my hand,
Never to draw it out, or manage arms
Against thyself or thy confederates,
But whilst I live will be at truce with thee.
ORC. But, Sigismund, confirm it with an oath,
And swear in sight of Heaven and by thy Christ.
SIG. By him that made the world and saved my soul,
The Son of God and issue of a Maid,
Sweet Jesus Christ, I solemnly protest
And vow to keep this peace inviolable.
ORC. By sacred Mahomet, the friend of God,
Whose holy Alcoran remains with us,
Whose glorious body, when he left the world,
Closed in a coffin mounted up the air,
And hung on stately Mecca's temple-roof,
I swear to keep this truce inviolable;
Of whose conditions and our solemn oaths,

6 Ready. Fr. *prêt*.

Signed with our hands, each shall retain a scroll
As memorable witness of our league.
Now, Sigismund, if any Christian king
Encroach upon the confines of thy realm,
Send word, Orcanes of Natolia
Confirmed this league beyond Danubius' stream,
And they will, trembling, sound a quick retreat;
So am I feared among all nations.

SIG. If any heathen potentate or king
Invade Natolia, Sigismund will send
A hundred thousand horse trained to the war,
And backed by stout lanciers of Germany,
The strength and sinews of the Imperial seat.

ORC. I thank thee, Sigismund; but, when I war,
All Asia Minor, Africa, and Greece,
Follow my standard and my thundering drums.
Come, let us go and banquet in our tents;
I will despatch chief of my army hence
To fair Natolia and to Trebizon,
To stay my coming 'gainst proud Tamburlaine.
Friend Sigismund, and peers of Hungary,
Come, banquet and carouse with us a while,
And then depart we to our territories. [*Exeunt.*

SCENE II.

Enter CALLAPINE *with* ALMEDA, *his Keeper.*

CALL. Sweet Almeda, pity the ruthful plight
Of Callapine, the son of Bajazeth,
Born to be monarch of the western world,
Yet here detained by cruel Tamburlaine.

ALM. My lord, I pity it, and with all my heart
Wish your release; but he whose wrath is death,
My sovereign lord, renownèd Tamburlaine,
Forbids you farther liberty than this.

CALL. Ah, were I now but half so eloquent
To paint in words what I'll perform in deeds,
I know thou would'st depart from hence with me.

ALM. Not for all Afric: therefore move me not.

CALL. Yet hear me speak, my gentle Almeda.

ALM. No speech to that end, by your favour, sir.

CALL. By Cairo runs——

ALM. No talk of running, I tell you, sir.
CALL. A little farther, gentle Almeda.
ALM. Well, sir, what of this?
CALL. By Cairo runs to Alexandria bay
Darote's streams, wherein at anchor lies
A Turkish galley of my royal fleet,
Waiting my coming to the river side,
Hoping by some means I shall be released,
Which, when I come aboard, will hoist up sail,
And soon put forth into the Terrene sea,
Where, 'twixt the isles of Cyprus and of Crete,
We quickly may in Turkish seas arrive.
Then shalt thou see a hundred kings and more,
Upon their knees, all bid me welcome home,
Amongst so many crowns of burnished gold,
Choose which thou wilt, all are at thy command;
A thousand galleys, manned with Christian slaves,
I freely give thee, which shall cut the Straits,
And bring armados from the coasts of Spain
Fraughted with gold of rich America;
The Grecian virgins shall attend on thee,
Skilful in music and in amorous lays,
As fair as was Pygmalion's ivory girl
Or lovely Iö metamorphosèd.
With naked negroes shall thy coach be drawn,
And as thou rid'st in triumph through the streets,
The pavement underneath thy chariot wheels
With Turkey carpets shall be coverèd,
And cloth of Arras hung about the walls,
Fit objects for thy princely eye to pierce.
A hundred bassoes, clothed in crimson silk,
Shall ride before thee on Barbarian steeds;
And when thou goest, a golden canopy
Enchased with precious stones, which shine as bright
As that fair veil that covers all the world,
When Phœbus, leaping from the hemisphere,
Descendeth downward to the Antipodes,
And more than this—for all I cannot tell.
ALM. How far hence lies the galley, say you?
CALL. Sweet Almeda, scarce half a league from hence.
ALM. But need[1] we not be spied going aboard?

---

1 Must.

CALL. Betwixt the hollow hanging of a hill,
And crookèd bending of a craggy rock,
The sails wrapt up, the mast and tacklings down,
She lies so close that none can find her out.

ALM. I like that well: but tell me, my lord, if I should let you go, would you be as good as your word? shall I be made a king for my labour?

CALL. As I am Callapine the Emperor,
And by the hand of Mahomet I swear
Thou shalt be crowned a king, and be my mate.

ALM. Then here I swear, as I am Almeda
Your keeper under Tamburlaine the Great,
(For that's the style and title I have yet),
Although he sent a thousand armèd men
To intercept this haughty enterprise,
Yet would I venture to conduct your grace,
And die before I brought you back again.

CALL. Thanks, gentle Almeda; then let us haste,
Lest time be past, and lingering let[2] us both.

ALM. When you will, my lord; I am ready.

CALL. Even straight; and farewell, cursèd Tamburlaine.
Now go I to revenge my father's death. [*Exeunt.*

SCENE III.

Enter TAMBURLAINE, ZENOCRATE, *and their three* Sons, CALYPHAS, AMYRAS, *and* CELEBINUS, *with drums and trumpets.*

TAMB. Now, bright Zenocrate, the world's fair eye,
Whose beams illuminate the lamps of Heaven,
Whose cheerful looks do clear the cloudy air,
And clothe it in a crystal livery;
Now rest thee here on fair Larissa plains,
Where Egypt and the Turkish empire part
Between thy sons, that shall be emperors,
And every one commander of a world.

ZENO. Sweet Tamburlaine, when wilt thou leave these arms,
And save thy sacred person free from scathe,
And dangerous chances of the wrathful war?

TAMB. When Heaven shall cease to move on both the poles,

---

2 Hinder.

And when the ground, whereon my soldiers march,
Shall rise aloft and touch the hornèd moon,
And not before, my sweet Zenocrate.
Sit up, and rest thee like a lovely queen;
So, now she sits in pomp and majesty,
When these, my sons, more precious in mine eyes,
Than all the wealthy kingdoms I subdued,
Placed by her side, look on their mother's face:
But yet methinks their looks are amorous,
Not martial as the sons of Tamburlaine:
Water and air, being symbolised in one,
Argue their want of courage and of wit;
Their hair as white as milk and soft as down,
(Which should be like the quills of porcupines
As black as jet and hard as iron or steel)
Bewrays they are too dainty for the wars;
Their fingers made to quaver on a lute,
Their arms to hang about a lady's neck,
Their legs to dance and caper in the air,
Would make me think them bastards not my sons,
But that I know they issued from thy womb
That never looked on man but Tamburlaine.

ZENO. My gracious lord, they have their mother's looks,
But when they list their conquering father's heart.
This lovely boy, the youngest of the three,
Not long ago bestrid a Scythian steed,
Trotting the ring, and tilting at a glove,
Which when he tainted[1] with his slender rod,
He reined him straight and made him so curvet,
As I cried out for fear he should have fallen.

TAMB. Well done, my boy, thou shalt have shield and lance,
Armour of proof, horse, helm, and curtle-axe,
And I will teach thee how to charge thy foe,
And harmless run among the deadly pikes.
If thou wilt love the wars and follow me,
Thou shalt be made a king and reign with me,
Keeping in iron cages emperors.
If thou exceed thy elder brothers' worth
And shine in còmplete virtue more than they,

1 Touched.

Thou shalt be king before them, and thy seed
Shall issue crownèd from their mother's womb.
CEL. Yes, father: you shall see me, if I live,
Have under me as many kings as you,
And march with such a multitude of men,
As all the world shall tremble at their view.
TAMB. These words assure me, boy, thou art my son.
When I am old and cannot manage arms,
Be thou the scourge and terror of the world.
AMY. Why may not I, my lord, as well as he,
Be termed the scourge and terror to the world?
TAMB. Be all a scourge and terror to the world,
Or else you are not sons of Tamburlaine.
CAL. But while my brothers follow arms, my lord,
Let me accompany my gracious mother;
They are enough to conquer all the world,
And you have won enough for me to keep.
TAMB. Bastardly boy, sprung from some coward's loins,
And not the issue of great Tamburlaine;
Of all the provinces I have subdued,
Thou shalt not have a foot unless thou bear
A mind courageous and invincible:
For he shall wear the crown of Persia
Whose head hath deepest scars, whose breast most wounds,
Which being wroth sends lightning from his eyes,
And in the furrows of his frowning brows
Harbours revenge, war, death, and cruelty;
For in a field, whose superficies
Is covered with a liquid purple veil
And sprinkled with the brains of slaughtered men,
My royal chair of state shall be advanced;
And he that means to place himself therein,
Must armèd wade up to the chin in blood.
ZENO. My lord, such speeches to our princely sons
Dismay their minds before they come to prove
The wounding troubles angry war affords.
CEL. No, madam, these are speeches fit for us,
For if his chair were in a sea of blood
I would prepare a ship and sail to it,
Ere I would lose the title of a king.
AMY. And I would strive to swim through pools of blood,

Or make a bridge of murdered carcases,
Whose arches should be framed with bones of Turks,
Ere I would lose the title of a king.
TAMB. Well, lovely boys, ye shall be emperors both,
Stretching your conquering arms from East to West;
And, sirrah, if you mean to wear a crown,
When we shall meet the Turkish deputy
And all his viceroys, snatch it from his head,
And cleave his pericraniun with thy sword.
CAL. If any man will hold him, I will strike
And cleave him to the channel[2] with my sword.
TAMB. Hold him, and cleave him too, or I'll cleave thee,
For we will march against them presently.
Theridamas, Techelles, and Casane
Promised to meet me on Larissa plains
With hosts apiece against this Turkish crew;
For I have sworn by sacred Mahomet
To make it parcel of my empery;
The trumpets sound, Zenocrate; they come.

Enter THERIDAMAS *and his* Train, *with drums and trumpets.*

TAMB. Welcome, Theridamas, King of Argier.
THER. My lord, the great and mighty Tamburlaine,—
Arch-monarch of the world, I offer here
My crown, myself, and all the power I have,
In all affection at thy kingly feet.
TAMB. Thanks, good Theridamas.
THER. Under my colours march ten thousand Greeks;
And of Argier's and Afric's frontier towns
Twice twenty thousand valiant men-at-arms,
All which have sworn to sack Natolia.
Five hundred brigandines are under sail,
Meet for your service on the sea, my lord,
That launching from Argier to Tripoli,
Will quickly ride before Natolia,
And batter down the castles on the shore.
TAMB. Well said, Argier; receive thy crown again.

Enter TECHELLES *and* USUMCASANE *together.*

TAMB. Kings of Moroccus and of Fez, welcome.

---

2 Collar-bone.

USUM. Magnificent and peerless Tamburlaine!
I and my neighbour King of Fez have brought
To aid thee in this Turkish expedition,
A hundred thousand expert soldiers:
From Azamor[3] to Tunis near the sea
Is Barbary unpeopled for thy sake,
And all the men in armour under me,
Which with my crown I gladly offer thee.
TAMB. Thanks, King of Moroccus, take your crown again.
TECH. And, mighty Tamburlaine, our earthly god,
Whose looks make this inferior world to quake,
I here present thee with the crown of Fez,
And with an host of Moors trained to the war,
Whose coal-black faces make their foes retire,
And quake for fear, as if infernal Jove
Meaning to aid thee in these Turkish arms,
Should pierce the black circumference of hell
With ugly Furies bearing fiery flags,
And millions of his strong tormenting spirits.
From strong Tesella unto Biledull
All Barbary is unpeopled for thy sake.
TAMB. Thanks, King of Fez; take here thy crown again.
Your presence, loving friends, and fellow kings,
Makes me to surfeit in conceiving joy.
If all the crystal gates of Jove's high court
Were opened wide, and I might enter in
To see the state and majesty of Heaven,
It could not more delight me than your sight.
Now will we banquet on these plains awhile,
And after march to Turkey with our camp,
In number more than are the drops that fall,
When Boreas rents a thousand swelling clouds;
And proud Orcanes of Natolia
With all his viceroys shall be so afraid,
That though the stones, as at Deucalion's flood,
Were turned to men, he should be overcome.
Such lavish will I make of Turkish blood,
That Jove shall send his wingèd messenger
To bid me sheath my sword and leave the field;
The sun unable to sustain the sight,

3 A maritime town of Morocco.

Shall hide his head in Thetis' watery lap,
And leave his steeds to fair Böotes' charge;
For half the world shall perish in this fight.
But now, my friends, let me examine ye;
How have ye spent your absent time from me?

USUM. My lord, our men of Barbary have marched
Four hundred miles with armour on their backs,
And lain in leaguer[4] fifteen months and more;
For, since we left you at the Soldan's court,
We have subdued the southern Guallatia,
And all the land unto the coast of Spain;
We kept the narrow Strait of Jubaltèr,
And made Canaria call us kings and lords;
Yet never did they recreate themselves,
Or cease one day from war and hot alarms,
And therefore let them rest awhile, my lord.

TAMB. They shall, Casane, and 'tis time, i' faith.

TECH. And I have marched along the river Nile
To Machda, where the mighty Christian priest,
Called John the Great,[5] sits in a milk-white robe,
Whose triple mitre I did take by force,
And made him swear obedience to my crown,
From thence unto Cazates did I march,
Where Amazonians met me in the field,
With whom, being women, I vouchsafed a league,
And with my power did march to Zanzibar,
The eastern part of Afric, where I viewed
The Ethiopian sea, rivers and lakes,
But neither man nor child in all the land;
Therefore I took my course to Manico,
Where unresisted, I removed my camp;
And by the coast of Byather, at last
I came to Cubar, where the negroes dwell,
And conquering that, made haste to Nubia.
There, having sacked Borno the kingly seat,
I took the king and led him bound in chains
Unto Damasco, where I stayed before.

TAMB. Well done, Techelles. What saith Theridamas?

THER. I left the confines and the bounds of Afric,
And thence I made a voyage into Europe,

---

4 The camp of a besieging force.
5 Prester John.

Where by the river Tyras I subdued
Stoka, Podolia, and Codemia;
Thence crossed the sea and came to Oblia
And Nigra Sylva, where the devils dance,
Which in despite of them, I set on fire.
From thence I crossed the gulf called by the name
Mare Majore[6] of the inhabitants.
Yet shall my soldiers make no period,
Until Natolia kneel before your feet.

TAMB. Then will we triumph, banquet and carouse;
Cooks shall have pensions to provide us cates
And glut us with the dainties of the world;
Lachryma Christi and Calabrian wines
Shall common soldiers drink in quaffing bowls,
Ay, liquid gold (when we have conquered him)
Mingled with coral and with orient pearl.
Come, let us banquet and carouse the whiles. [*Exeunt*.

6 The old name of the Black Sea. So called by Marco Polo.

ACT THE SECOND.

Scene I.

Enter Sigismund, Frederick, Baldwin, *and their* Train.

Sig. Now say, my lords of Buda and Bohemia,
What motion is it that inflames your thoughts,
And stirs your valours to such sudden arms?

Fred. Your majesty remembers, I am sure,
What cruel slaughter of our Christian bloods
These heathenish Turks and Pagans lately made,
Betwixt the city Zula and Danubius;
How through the midst of Varna and Bulgaria,
And almost to the very walls of Rome,
They have, not long since, massacred our camp.
It resteth now, then, that your majesty
Take all advantages of time and power,
And work revenge upon these infidels.
Your highness knows, for Tamburlaine's repair,
That strikes a terror to all Turkish hearts,
Natolia hath dismissed the greatest part
Of all his army, pitched against our power,
Betwixt Cutheia and Orminius' mount,[1]
And sent them marching up to Belgasar,
Acantha,[2] Antioch, and Cæsarea,
To aid the Kings of Soria, and Jerusalem.
Now then, my lord, advantage take thereof,
And issue suddenly upon the rest;
That in the fortune of their overthrow,

1 Probably Armenyes, in Transylvania.
2 Acanthus, near Mount Athos.

We may discourage all the pagan troop,
That dare attempt to war with Christians.

SIG. But calls not then your grace to memory
The league we lately made with King Orcanes,
Confirmed by oath and articles of peace,
And calling Christ for record of our truths?
This should be treachery and violence
Against the grace of our profession.

BALD. No whit, my lord, for with such infidels,
In whom no faith nor true religion rests,
We are not bound to those accomplishments
The holy laws of Christendom enjoin;
But as the faith, which they profanely plight,
Is not by necessary policy
To be esteemed assurance for ourselves,
So that we vow to them should not infringe
Our liberty of arms or victory.

SIG. Though I confess the oaths they undertake
Breed little strength to our security.
Yet those infirmities that thus defame
Their faiths, their honours, and their religion,
Should not give us presumption to the like.
Our faiths are sound, and must be consummate,
Religious, righteous, and inviolate.

FRED. Assure your grace, 'tis superstition
To stand so strictly on dispensive faith;
And should we lose the opportunity
That God hath given to venge our Christians' death,
And scourge their foul blasphèmous Paganism,
As fell to Saul, to Balaam, and the rest,
That would not kill and curse at God's command,
So surely will the vengeance of the Highest,
And jealous anger of His fearful arm,
Be poured with rigour on our sinful heads,
If we neglect this offered victory.

SIG. Then arm, my lords, and issue suddenly,
Giving commandment to our general host,
With expedition to assail the Pagan,
And take the victory our God hath given. [*Exeunt*.

Scene II.

Enter Orcanes, Gazellus, Uribassa, *with their* Trains.

Orc. Gazellus, Uribassa, and the rest,
Now will we march from proud Orminius' mount,
To fair Natolia, where our neighbour kings
Expect our power and our royal presence,
To encounter with the cruel Tamburlaine,
That nigh Larissa sways a mighty host,
And with the thunder of his martial tools
Makes earthquakes in the hearts of men and Heaven.
Gaz. And now come we to make his sinews shake,
With greater power than erst his pride hath felt.
An hundred kings, by scores, will bid him arms,
And hundred thousands subjects to each score,
Which, if a shower of wounding thunderbolts
Should break out of the bowels of the clouds,
And fall as thick as hail upon our heads,
In partial aid of that proud Scythian,
Yet should our courages and steelèd crests,
And numbers, more than infinite, of men,
Be able to withstand and conquer him.
Uri. Methinks I see how glad the Christian king
Is made, for joy of your admitted truce,
That could not but before be terrified
With unacquainted power of our host.

Enter a Messenger.

Mess. Arm, dread sovereign, and my noble lords!
The treacherous army of the Christians,
Taking advantage of your slender power,
Comes marching on us, and determines straight
To bid us battle for our dearest lives.
Orc. Traitors! villains! damnèd Christians!
Have I not here the articles of peace,
And solemn covenants we have both confirmed,
He by his Christ, and I by Mahomet?
Gaz. Hell and confusion light upon their heads,
That with such treason seek our overthrow,
And care so little for their prophet, Christ!
Orc. Can there be such deceit in Christians,
Or treason in the fleshly heart of man,

Whose shape is figure of the highest God!
Then, if there be a Christ, as Christians say,
But in their deeds deny him for their Christ,
If he be son to everliving Jove,
And hath the power of his outstretchèd arm;
If he be jealous of his name and honour,
As is our holy prophet, Mahomet;—
Take here these papers as our sacrifice
And witness of thy servant's perjury.
[*He tears to pieces the articles of peace.*
Open, thou shining veil of Cynthia,
And make a passage from the empyreal Heaven,
That he that sits on high and never sleeps,
Nor in one place is circumscriptible,
But everywhere fills every continent
With strange infusion of his sacred vigour,
May, in his endless power and purity,
Behold and venge this traitor's perjury!
Thou Christ, that art esteemed omnipotent,
If thou wilt prove thyself a perfect God,
Worthy the worship of all faithful hearts,
Be now revenged upon this traitor's soul,
And make the power I have left behind,
(Too little to defend our guiltless lives),
Sufficient to discomfort and confound
The trustless force of those false Christians.
To arms, my lords! On Christ still let us cry!
If there be Christ, we shall have victory.

SCENE III.

Alarms of battle within.—Enter SIGISMUND, *wounded.*

SIG. Discomfited is all the Christian host,
And God hath thundered vengeance from on high,
For my accursed and hateful perjury.
O, just and dreadful punisher of sin,
Let the dishonour of the pains I feel,
In this my mortal well-deservèd wound,
End all my penance in my sudden death!
And let this death, wherein to sin I die,
Conceive a second life in endless mercy! [*He dies.*

Enter ORCANES, GAZELLUS, URIBASSA, *and others.*

ORC. Now lie the Christians bathing in their bloods,
And Christ or Mahomet hath been my friend.
GAZ. See here the perjured traitor Hungary,
Bloody and breathless for his villainy.
ORC. Now shall his barbarous body be a prey
To beasts and fowls, and all the winds shall breathe
Through shady leaves of every senseless tree
Murmurs and hisses for his heinous sin.
Now scalds his soul in the Tartarian streams,
And feeds upon the baneful tree of hell,
That Zoacum,[1] that fruit of bitterness,
That in the midst of fire is ingraffed,
Yet flourishes as Flora in her pride,
With apples like the heads of damnèd fiends.
The devils there, in chains of quenchless flame,
Shall lead his soul through Orcus' burning gulf,
From pain to pain, whose change shall never end.
What say'st thou yet, Gazellus, to his foil,
Which we referred to justice of his Christ,
And to his power, which here appears as full
As rays of Cynthia to the clearest sight?
GAZ. 'Tis but the fortune of the wars, my lord,
Whose power is often proved a miracle.
ORC. Yet in my thoughts shall Christ be honourèd,
Not doing Mahomet an injury,
Whose power had share in this our victory;
And since this miscreant hath disgraced his faith
And died a traitor both to Heaven and earth,
We will both watch and ward shall keep his trunk
Amidst these plains for fowls to prey upon.
Go, Uribassa, give it straight in charge.
URI. I will, my lord. [*Exit.*
ORC. And now, Gazellus, let us haste and meet
Our army, and our brothers of Jerusalem,
Of Soria, Trebizon, and Amasia,
And happily, with full Natolian bowls
Of Greekish wine, now let us celebrate
Our happy conquest and his angry fate. [*Exeunt.*

---

1 The description of this tree is taken from the Koran, Chap. 37.

Scene IV.

ZENOCRATE *is discovered lying in her bed of state, with* TAMBURLAINE *sitting by her. About her bed are three* PHYSICIANS *tempering potions. Around are* THERIDAMAS, TECHELLES, USUMCASANE, *and her three Sons.*

TAMB. Black is the beauty of the brightest day;
The golden ball of Heaven's eternal fire,
That danced with glory on the silver waves,
Now wants the fuel that inflamed his beams;
And all with faintness, and for foul disgrace,
He binds his temples with a frowning cloud,
Ready to darken earth with endless night.
Zenocrate, that gave him light and life,
Whose eyes shot fire from their ivory bowers
And tempered every soul with lively heat,
Now by the malice of the angry skies,
Whose jealousy admits no second mate,
Draws in the comfort of her latest breath,
All dazzled with the hellish mists of death.
Now walk the angels on the walls of Heaven,
As sentinels to warn the immortal souls
To entertain divine Zenocrate.
Apollo, Cynthia, and the ceaseless lamps
That gently looked upon this loathsome earth,
Shine downward now no more, but deck the Heavens
To entertain divine Zenocrate.
The crystal springs, whose taste illuminates
Refinèd eyes with an eternal sight,
Like trièd silver run through Paradise
To entertain divine Zenocrate.
The cherubins and holy seraphins,
That sing and play before the King of kings,
Use all their voices and their instruments
To entertain divine Zenocrate.
And in this sweet and curious harmony,
The God that tunes this music to our souls,
Holds out his hand in highest majesty
To entertain divine Zenocrate.
Then let some holy trance convey my thoughts
Up to the palace of th' empyreal Heaven,

That this my life may be as short to me
As are the days of sweet Zenocrate.—
Physicians, will no physic do her good?
PHYS. My lord, your majesty shall soon perceive:
And if she pass this fit, the worst is past.
TAMB. Tell me, how fares my fair Zenocrate?
ZENO. I fare, my lord, as other empresses,
That, when this frail and transitory flesh
Hath sucked the measure of that vital air
That feeds the body with his dated health,
Wade with enforced and necessary change.
TAMB. May never such a change transform my love,
In whose sweet being I repose my life,
Whose heavenly presence, beautified with health,
Gives light to Phoebus and the fixèd stars!
Whose absence makes the sun and moon as dark
As when, opposed in one diameter,
Their spheres are mounted on the serpent's head,
Or else descended to his winding train.
Live still, my love, and so conserve my life,
Or, dying, be the author of my death!
ZENO. Live still, my lord! O, let my sovereign live
And sooner let the fiery element
Dissolve and make your kingdom in the sky,
Than this base earth should shroud your majesty:
For should I but suspect your death by mine,
The comfort of my future happiness,
And hope to meet your highness in the Heavens,
Turned to despair, would break my wretched breast,
And fury would confound my present rest.
But let me die, my love; yet let me die;
With love and patience let your true love die!
Your grief and fury hurts my second life.—
Yet let me kiss my lord before I die,
And let me die with kissing of my lord.
But since my life is lengthened yet a while,
Let me take leave of these my loving sons,
And of my lords, whose true nobility
Have merited my latest memory.
Sweet sons, farewell! In death resemble me,
And in your lives your father's excellence.
Some music, and my fit will cease, my lord.
[*They call for music.*

TAMB. Proud fury, and intolerable fit,
That dares torment the body of my love,
And scourge the scourge of the immortal God:
Now are those spheres, where Cupid used to sit,
Wounding the world with wonder and with love,
Sadly supplied with pale and ghastly death,
Whose darts do pierce the centre of my soul.
Her sacred beauty hath enchanted Heaven;
And had she lived before the siege of Troy,
Helen (whose beauty summoned Greece to arms;
And drew a thousand ships to Tenedos)[1]
Had not been named in Homer's Iliad;
Her name had been in every line he wrote.
Or had those wanton poets, for whose birth
Old Rome was proud, but gazed a while on her,
Nor Lesbia nor Corinna had been named;
Zenocrate had been the argument
Of every epigram or elegy.

[*The music sounds.*—ZENOCRATE *dies.*

What, is she dead? Techelles, draw thy sword
And wound the earth, that it may cleave in twain,
And we descend into the infernal vaults,
To hale the Fatal Sisters by the hair,
And throw them in the triple moat of hell,
For taking hence my fair Zenocrate.
Casane and Theridamas, to arms!
Raise cavalieros[2] higher than the clouds,
And with the cannon break the frame of Heaven;
Batter the shining palace of the sun,
And shiver all the starry firmament,
For amorous Jove hath snatched my love from hence,
Meaning to make her stately queen of Heaven.
What god soever holds thee in his arms,
Giving thee nectar and ambrosia,
Behold me here, divine Zenocrate,
Raving, impatient, desperate, and mad,
Breaking my steelèd lance, with which I burst
The rusty beams of Janus' temple-doors,
Letting out Death and tyrannising War,

1 "Was this the face that launched a thousand ships?" See "*Doctor Faustus*," scene xiv.
2 *Cavalier* was a word used for a mound for cannons elevated above the rest of the works of a fortress.

To march with me under this bloody flag!
And if thou pitiest Tamburlaine the Great,
Come down from Heaven, and live with me again!

THER. Ah, good my lord, be patient; she is dead,
And all this raging cannot make her live.
If words might serve, our voice hath rent the air;
If tears, our eyes have watered all the earth;
If grief, our murdered hearts have strained forth blood;
Nothing prevails, for she is dead, my lord.

TAMB. "For she is dead!" Thy words do pierce my soul!
Ah, sweet Theridamas! say so no more;
Though she be dead, yet let me think she lives,
And feed my mind that dies for want of her.
Where'er her soul be, thou [*To the body*] shalt stay with me,
Embalmed with cassia, ambergris, and myrrh,
Not lapt in lead, but in a sheet of gold,
And till I die thou shalt not be interred.
Then in as rich a tomb as Mausolus'
We both will rest and have one epitaph
Writ in as many several languages
As I have conquered kingdoms with my sword.
This cursèd town will I consume with fire,
Because this place bereaved me of my love:
The houses, burnt, will look as if they mourned;
And here will I set up her statua,
And march about it with my mourning camp
Drooping and pining for Zenocrate. [*The scene closes.*

ACT THE THIRD.

SCENE I.

Enter the KINGS *of* TREBIZON *and* SORIA, *one bearing a sword, and the other a sceptre; next* ORCANES King *of* Natolia *and the* KING *of* JERUSALEM *with the imperial crown; after them enters* CALLAPINE, *and after him other* Lords *and* ALMEDA. ORCANES *and the* KING *of* JERUSALEM *crown* CALLAPINE, *and the others give him the sceptre.*

ORC. Callapinus Cyricelibes, otherwise Cybelius, son and successive heir to the late mighty emperor, Bajazeth, by the aid of God and his friend Mahomet, Emperor of Natolia, Jerusalem, Trebizond, Soria, Amasia, Thracia, Illyria, Carmania, and all the hundred and thirty kingdoms late contributory to his mighty father. Long live Callapinus, Emperor of Turkey!

CALL. Thrice worthy kings of Natolia, and the rest,
I will requite your royal gratitudes
With all the benefits my empire yields;
And were the sinews of the imperial seat
So knit and strengthened as when Bajazeth
My royal lord and father filled the throne,
Whose cursèd fate hath so dismembered it,
Then should you see this thief of Scythia,
This proud, usurping King of Persia,
Do us such honour and supremacy,
Bearing the vengeance of our father's wrongs,
As all the world should blot his dignities
Out of the book of base-born infamies.
And now I doubt not but your royal cares
Hath so provided for this cursèd foe,
That, since the heir of mighty Bajazeth,
(An emperor so honoured for his virtues),
Revives the spirits of all true Turkish hearts,

In grievous memory of his father's shame,
We shall not need to nourish any doubt,
But that proud fortune, who hath followed long
The martial sword of mighty Tamburlaine,
Will now retain her old inconstancy
And raise our honours to as high a pitch,
In this our strong and fortunate encounter;
For so hath Heaven provided my escape,
From all the cruelty my soul sustained,
By this my friendly keeper's happy means,
That Jove, surcharged with pity of our wrongs,
Will pour it down in showers on our heads,
Scourging the pride of cursèd Tamburlaine.

ORC. I have a hundred thousand men in arms;
Some, that in conquest of the perjured Christian,
Being a handful to a mighty host,
Think them in number yet sufficient
To drink the river Nile or Euphrates,
And for their power enow to win the world.

K. OF JER. And I as many from Jerusalem,
Judæa, Gaza, and Scalonia's[1] bounds,
That on Mount Sinai with their ensigns spread,
Look like the parti-coloured clouds of Heaven
That show fair weather to the neighbour morn.

K. OF TREB. And I as many bring from Trebizond,
Chio, Famastro, and Amasia,
All bordering on the Mare Major sea,[2]
Riso,[3] Sancina, and the bordering towns
That touch the end of famous Euphrates,
Whose courages are kindled with the flames,
The cursed Scythian sets on all their towns,
And vow to burn the villain's cruel heart.

K. OF SOR. From Soria with seventy thousand strong
Ta'en from Aleppo, Soldino, Tripoli,
And so on to my city of Damasco,
I march to meet and aid my neighbour kings;
All which will join against this Tamburlaine,
And bring him captive to your highness' feet.

ORC. Our battle then in martial manner pitched,

---

1 Scalonia, *i.e.* Ascalon.
2 The Black Sea.
3 Evidently Rizeli, a town near Trebizond.

According to our ancient use, shall bear
The figure of the semicircled moon,
Whose horns shall sprinkle through the tainted air
The poisoned brains of this proud Scythian.

CALL. Well then, my noble lords, for this my friend
That freed me from the bondage of my foe,
I think it requisite and honourable,
To keep my promise and to make him king,
That is a gentleman, I know, at least.

ALM. That's no matter, sir, for being a king; for
Tamburlaine came up of nothing.

K. OF JER. Your majesty may choose some 'pointed time,
Performing all your promise to the full;
'Tis nought for your majesty to give a kingdom.

CALL. Then will I shortly keep my promise, Almeda.

ALM. Why, I thank your majesty. [*Exeunt.*

SCENE II.

Enter TAMBURLAINE, *with his three* Sons *and* USUMCASANE; *four* Attendants *bearing the hearse of* ZENOCRATE; *the drums sounding a doleful march; the town burning.*

TAMB. So burn the turrets of this cursèd town,
Flame to the highest region of the air,
And kindle heaps of exhalations
That being fiery meteors may presage
Death and destruction to the inhabitants!
Over my zenith hang a blazing star,
That may endure till Heaven be dissolved,
Fed with the fresh supply of earthly dregs,
Threatening a death and famine to this land!
Flying dragons, lightning, fearful thunderclaps,
Singe these fair plains, and make them seem as black
As is the island where the Furies mask,
Compassed with Lethe, Styx, and Phlegethon,
Because my dear'st Zenocrate is dead.

CAL. This pillar, placed in memory of her,
Where in Arabian, Hebrew, Greek, is writ:—
This town, being burnt by Tamburlaine the Great,
Forbids the world to build it up again.

AMY. And here this mournful streamer shall be placed,
Wrought with the Persian and th' Egyptian arms,

To signify she was a princess born,
And wife unto the monarch of the East.
CEL. And here this table as a register
Of all her virtues and perfections.
TAMB. And here the picture of Zenocrate,
To show her beauty which the world admired;
Sweet picture of divine Zenocrate,
That, hanging here, will draw the gods from Heaven,
And cause the stars fixed in the southern arc,
(Whose lovely faces never any viewed
That have not passed the centre's latitude),
As pilgrims, travel to our hemisphere,
Only to gaze upon Zenocrate.
Thou shalt not beautify Larissa plains,
But keep within the circle of mine arms.
At every town and castle I besiege,
Thou shalt be set upon my royal tent;
And when I meet an army in the field,
Those looks will shed such influence in my camp
As if Bellona, goddess of the war,
Threw naked swords and sulphur-balls of fire
Upon the heads of all our enemies.
And now, my lords, advance your spears again:
Sorrow no more, my sweet Casane, now;
Boys, leave to mourn! this town shall ever mourn,
Being burnt to cinders for your mother's death.
CAL. If I had wept a sea of tears for her,
It would not ease the sorrows I sustain.
AMY. As is that town, so is my heart consumed
With grief and sorrow for my mother's death.
CEL. My mother's death hath mortified my mind,
And sorrow stops the passage of my speech.
TAMB. But now, my boys, leave off and list to me.
That mean to teach you rudiments of war;
I'll have you learn to sleep upon the ground,
March in your armour thorough watery fens,
Sustain the scorching heat and freezing cold,
Hunger and thirst, right adjuncts of the war,
And after this to scale a castle wall,
Besiege a fort, to undermine a town,
And make whole cities caper in the air.
Then next the way to fortify your men,
In champion grounds, what figure serves you best,

For which the quinque-angle form is meet,
Because the corners there may fall more flat
Whereas the fort may fittest be assailed,
And sharpest where the assault is desperate.
The ditches must be deep; the counterscarps[1]
Narrow and steep; the walls made high and broad;
The bulwarks and the rampires large and strong,
With cavalieros and thick counterforts,
And room within to lodge six thousand men.
It must have privy ditches, countermines,
And secret issuings to defend the ditch;
It must have high argins[2] and covered ways,
To keep the bulwark fronts from battery,
And parapets to hide the musketers;
Casemates to place the great artillery;
And store of ordnance, that from every flank
May scour the outward curtains of the fort,
Dismount the cannon of the adverse part,
Murder the foe, and save the walls from breach.
When this is learned for service on the land,
By plain and easy demonstration
I'll teach you how to make the water mount,
That you may dry-foot march through lakes and pools,
Deep rivers, havens, creeks, and little seas,
And make a fortress in the raging waves,
Fenced with the concave of monstrous rock,
Invincible by nature of the place.
When this is done then are ye soldiers,
And worthy sons of Tamburlaine the Great.

CAL. My lord, but this is dangerous to be done;
We may be slain or wounded ere we learn.

TAMB. Villain! art thou the son of Tamburlaine,
And fear'st to die, or with a curtle-axe
To hew thy flesh, and make a gaping wound?
Hast thou beheld a peal of ordnance strike
A ring of pikes, mingled with shot[3] and horse,
Whose shattered limbs, being tossed as high as Heaven,
Hang in the air as thick as sunny motes,
And canst thou, coward, stand in fear of death?

---

1 That side of the ditch nearest the besiegers.
2 *Argine* (Ital.) earthworks.
3 "Mingled with *shot*" means with musketeers.

Hast thou not seen my horsemen charge the foe,
Shot through the arms, cut overthwart the hands,
Dyeing their lances with their streaming blood,
And yet at night carouse within my tent,
Filling their empty veins with airy wine,
That, being concocted, turns to crimson blood,
And wilt thou shun the field for fear of wounds?
View me, thy father, that hath conquered kings,
And, with his horse, marched round about the earth,
Quite void of scars, and clear from any wound,
That by the wars lost not a drop of blood,
And see him lance his flesh to teach you all.

[*He cuts his arm.*

A wound is nothing, be it ne'er so deep;
Blood is the god of war's rich livery.
Now look I like a soldier, and this wound
As great a grace and majesty to me,
As if a chain of gold enamellèd,
Enchased with diamonds, sapphires, rubies,
And fairest pearl of wealthy India,
Were mounted here under a canopy,
And I sate down clothed with a massy robe,
That late adorned the Afric potentate,
Whom I brought bound unto Damascus' walls.
Come, boys, and with your fingers search my wound,
And in my blood wash all your hands at once,
While I sit smiling to behold the sight.
Now, my boys, what think ye of a wound?

CAL. I know not what I should think of it; methinks it is a pitiful sight.

CEL. 'Tis nothing: Give me a wound, father.

AMY. And me another, my lord.

TAMB. Come, sirrah, give me your arm.

CEL. Here, father, cut it bravely, as you did your own.

TAMB. It shall suffice thou darest abide a wound;
My boy, thou shalt not lose a drop of blood
Before we meet the army of the Turk:
But then run desperate through the thickest throngs,
Dreadless of blows, of bloody wounds, and death;
And let the burning of Larissa-walls,
My speech of war, and this my wound you see,
Teach you, my boys, to bear courageous minds,
Fit for the followers of great Tamburlaine!

Usumcasane, now come let us march
Towards Techelles and Theridamas,
That we have sent before to fire the towns
The towers and cities of these hateful Turks,
And hunt that coward faint-heart runaway,
With that accursèd traitor Almeda,
Till fire and sword have found them at a bay.

USUM. I long to pierce his bowels with my sword,
That hath betrayed my gracious sovereign,—
That cursed and damnèd traitor Almeda.

TAMB. Then let us see if coward Callapine
Dare levy arms against our puissance,
That we may tread upon his captive neck,
And treble all his father's slaveries. [*Exeunt.*

SCENE III.

Enter TECHELLES, THERIDAMAS, *and their* Train.

THER. Thus have we marched northward from Tamburlaine,
Unto the frontier point of Soria;
And this is Balsera, their chiefest hold,[1]
Wherein is all the treasure of the land.

TECH. Then let us bring our light artillery,
Minions, falc'nets, and sakers[2] to the trench,
Filling the ditches with the walls' wide breach,
And enter in to seize upon the hold.
How say you, soldiers? shall we or not?

SOLD. Yes, my lord, yes; come, let's about it.

THER. But stay awhile; summon a parley, drum.
It may be they will yield it quietly,
Knowing two kings, the friends to Tamburlaine,
Stand at the walls with such a mighty power.

A *parley sounded.—The* CAPTAIN *appears on the walls, with* OLYMPIA *his* Wife, *and his* Son.

CAPT. What require you, my masters?

THER. Captain, that thou yield up thy hold to us.

CAPT. To you! Why, do you think me weary of it?

---

1 Fortress.
2 These were all small pieces of ordnance.

TECH. Nay, captain, thou art weary of thy life,
If thou withstand the friends of Tamburlaine!
THER. These pioners of Argier in Africa,
Even in the cannon's face, shall raise a hill
Of earth and faggots higher than the fort,
And over thy argins and covered ways
Shall play upon the bulwarks of thy hold
Volleys of ordnance, till the breach be made
That with his ruin fills up all the trench,
And when we enter in, not Heaven itself
Shall ransom thee, thy wife, and family.
TECH. Captain, these Moors shall cut the leaden pipes,
That bring fresh water to thy men and thee,
And lie in trench before thy castle walls,
That no supply of victual shall come in,
Nor any issue forth but they shall die;
And, therefore, captain, yield it quietly.
CAPT. Were you, that are the friends of Tamburlaine,
Brothers of holy Mahomet himself,
I would not yield it; therefore do your worst:
Raise mounts, batter, intrench, and undermine,
Cut off the water, all convoys that come,
Yet I am resolute, and so farewell.

[CAPTAIN, OLYMPIA, *and their* Son *retire from the walls.*

THER. Pioners, away! and where I stuck the stake,
Intrench with those dimensions I prescribed.
Cast up the earth towards the castle wall,
Which, till it may defend you, labour low,
And few or none shall perish by their shot.
PIO. We will, my lord. [*Exeunt* Pioners.
TECH. A hundred horse shall scout about the plains
To spy what force comes to relieve the hold.
Both we, Theridamas, will entrench our men,
And with the Jacob's staff[3] measure the height
And distance of the castle from the trench,
That we may know if our artillery
Will carry full point-blank unto their walls.
THER. Then see the bringing of our ordnance
Along the trench into the battery,

3 A mathematical instrument.

Where we will have gabions of six feet broad
To save our cannoniers from musket shot.
Betwixt which shall our ordnance thunder forth,
And with the breach's fall, smoke, fire, and dust,
The crack, the echo, and the soldier's cry,
Make deaf the ear and dim the crystal sky.

TECH. Trumpets and drums, alarum presently;
And, soldiers, play the men; the hold is yours. [*Exeunt.*

SCENE IV.

Alarm within.—Enter the CAPTAIN, *with* OLYMPIA, *and his* Son.

OLYMP. Come, good my lord, and let us haste from hence
Along the cave that leads beyond the foe;
No hope is left to save this conquered hold.

CAPT. A deadly bullet, gliding through my side,
Lies heavy on my heart; I cannot live.
I feel my liver pierced, and all my veins,
That there begin and nourish every part,
Mangled and torn, and all my entrails bathed
In blood that straineth from their orifex.
Farewell, sweet wife! sweet son, farewell! I die. [*He dies.*

OLYMP. Death, whither art thou gone, that both we live?
Come back again, sweet Death, and strike us both!
One minute end our days! and one sepùlchre
Contain our bodies! Death, why com'st thou not?
Well, this must be the messenger for thee:
[*Drawing a dagger.*
Now, ugly Death, stretch out thy sable wings,
And carry both our souls where his remains.
Tell me, sweet boy, art thou content to die?
These barbarous Scythians, full of cruelty,
And Moors, in whom was never pity found,
Will hew us piecemeal, put us to the wheel,
Or else invent some torture worse than that;
Therefore die by thy loving mother's hand,
Who gently now will lance thy ivory throat,
And quickly rid thee both of pain and life.

SON. Mother, despatch me, or I'll kill myself;
For think you I can live and see him dead?
Give me your knife, good mother, or strike home:

The Scythians shall not tyrannise on me:
Sweet mother, strike, that I may meet my father.
[*She stabs him and he dies.*

OLYMP. Ah, sacred Mahomet, if this be sin,
Entreat a pardon of the God of Heaven,
And purge my soul before it comes to thee.
[*She burns the bodies of her* Husband *and* Son *and then attempts to kill herself.*

Enter THERIDAMAS, TECHELLES, *and all their* Train.

THER. How now, madam, what are you doing?
OLYMP. Killing myself, as I have done my son,
Whose body, with his father's, I have burnt,
Lest cruel Scythians should dismember him.
TECH. 'Twas bravely done, and, like a soldier's wife.
Thou shalt with us to Tamburlaine the Great,
Who, when he hears how resolute thou art,
Will match thee with a viceroy or a king.
OLYMP. My lord deceased was dearer unto me
Than any viceroy, king, or emperor;
And for his sake here will I end my days.
THER. But, lady, go with us to Tamburlaine,
And thou shalt see a man, greater than Mahomet,
In whose high looks is much more majesty
Than from the concave superficies
Of Jove's vast palace, the empyreal orb,
Unto the shining bower where Cynthia sits,
Like lovely Thetis, in a crystal robe;
That treadeth fortune underneath his feet,
And makes the mighty God of arms his slave;
On whom Death and the Fatal Sisters wait
With naked swords and scarlet liveries:
Before whom, mounted on a lion's back,
Rhamnusia bears a helmet full of blood,
And strews the way with brains of slaughtered men;
By whose proud side the ugly Furies run,
Hearkening when he shall bid them plague the world;
Over whose zenith, clothed in windy air,
And eagle's wings joined to her feathered breast,
Fame hovereth, sounding of her golden trump,
That to the adverse poles of that straight line,
Which measureth the glorious frame of Heaven,
The name of mighty Tamburlaine is spread,

And him, fair lady, shall thy eyes behold.
Come!

OLYMP. Take pity of a lady's ruthful tears,
That humbly craves upon her knees to stay
And cast her body in the burning flame,
That feeds upon her son's and husband's flesh.

TECH. Madam, sooner shall fire consume us both,
Than scorch a face so beautiful as this,
In frame of which Nature hath showed more skill
Than when she gave eternal chaos form,
Drawing from it the shining lamps of Heaven.

THER. Madam, I am so far in love with you,
That you must go with us—no remedy.

OLYMP. Then carry me, I care not, where you will,
And let the end of this my fatal journey
Be likewise end to my accursèd life.

TECH. No, madam, but the beginning of your joy:
Come willingly therefore.

THER. Soldiers, now let us meet the general,
Who by this time is at Natolia,
Ready to charge the army of the Turk.
The gold and silver, and the pearl, we got,
Rifling this fort, divide in equal shares:
This lady shall have twice as much again
Out of the coffers of our treasury. [*Exeunt.*

SCENE V.

Enter CALLAPINE, ORCANES, ALMEDA, *and the* KINGS *of* JERUSALEM, TREBIZOND, *and* SORIA, *with their* Trains—*To them enters a* Messenger.

MES. Renownèd emperor, mighty Callapine,
God's great lieutenant over all the world!
Here at Aleppo, with a host of men,
Lies Tamburlaine, this King of Persia,
(in numbers more than are the quivering leaves
Of Ida's forest, where your highness' hounds,
With open cry, pursue the wounded stag),
Who means to girt Natolia's walls with siege,
Fire the town, and overrun the land.

CALL. My royal army is as great as his,
That, from the bounds of Phrygia to the sea

Which washeth Cyprus with his brinish waves,
Covers the hills, the valleys, and the plains.
Viceroys and peers of Turkey, play the men!
Whet all your swords to mangle Tamburlaine,
His sons, his captains, and his followers;
By Mahomet! not one of them shall live;
The field wherein this battle shall be fought
For ever term the Persian's sepulchre,
In memory of this our victory!

ORC. Now, he that calls himself the scourge of Jove,
The emperor of the world, and earthly god,
Shall end the warlike progress he intends,
And travel headlong to the lake of hell,
Where legions of devils, (knowing he must die
Here, in Natolia, by your highness' hands),
All brandishing their brands of quenchless fire,
Stretching their monstrous paws, grin with their teeth
And guard the gates to entertain his soul.

CALL. Tell me, viceroys, the number of your men,
And what our army royal is esteemed.

K. OF JER. From Palestina and Jerusalem,
Of Hebrews threescore thousand fighting men
Are come since last we showed your majesty.

ORC. So from Arabia Desert, and the bounds
Of that sweet land, whose brave metropolis
Re-edified the fair Semiramis,
Came forty thousand warlike foot and horse,
Since last we numbered to your majesty.

K. OF TREB. From Trebizond, in Asia the Less,
Naturalised Turks and stout Bithynians
Came to my bands, full fifty thousand more
(That, fighting, know not what retreat doth mean,
Nor e'er return but with the victory),
Since last we numbered to your majesty.

K. OF SOR. Of Sorians from Halla is repaired,
And neighbour cities of your highness' land,
Ten thousand horse, and thirty thousand foot,
Since last we numbered to your majesty;
So that the army royal is esteemed
Six hundred thousand valiant fighting men.

CALL. Then welcome, Tamburlaine, unto thy death.
Come, puissant viceroys, let us to the field,
(The Persians' sepulchre), and sacrifice
Mountains of breathless men to Mahomet,

Who now, with Jove, opens the firmament
To see the slaughter of our enemies.

Enter TAMBURLAINE *with his three* Sons, USUMCASANE, *and others.*

TAMB. How now, Casane? See a knot of kings,
Sitting as if they were a-telling riddles.
USUM. My lord, your presence makes them pale and wan:
Poor souls! they look as if their deaths were near.
TAMB. And so he is, Casane; I am here;
But yet I'll save their lives, and make them slaves.
Ye petty kings of Turkey, I am come,
As Hector did into the Grecian camp,
To overdare the pride of Græcia
And set his warlike person to the view
Of fierce Achilles, rival of his fame:
I do you honour in the simile;
For if I should, as Hector did Achilles,
(The worthiest knight that ever brandished sword)
Challenge in combat any of you all,
I see how fearfully ye would refuse,
And fly my glove as from a scorpion.
ORC. Now thou art fearful of thy army's strength,
Thou would'st with overmatch of person fight;
But, shepherd's issue, base-born Tamburlaine,
Think of thy end! this sword shall lance thy throat.
TAMB. Villain! the shepherd's issue (at whose birth
Heaven did afford a gracious aspèct,
And joined those stars that shall be opposite
Even till the dissolution of the world,
And never meant to make a conqueror
So famous as is mighty Tamburlaine),
Shall so torment thee and that Callapine,
That, like a roguish runaway, suborned
That villain there, that slave, that Turkish dog,
To false his service to his sovereign,
As ye shall curse the birth of Tamburlaine.
CALL. Rail not, proud Scythian! I shall now revenge
My father's vile abuses, and mine own.
K. OF JER. By Mahomet! he shall be tied in chains,
Rowing with Christians in a brigandine
About the Grecian isles to rob and spoil,
And turn him to his ancient trade again:
Methinks the slave should make a lusty thief.

CALL. Nay, when the battle ends, all we will meet,
And sit in council to invent some pain
That most may vex his body and his soul.
TAMB. Sirrah, Callapine! I'll hang a clog about
your neck for running away again; you shall not
trouble me thus to come and fetch you;
But as for you, viceroy, you shall have bits,
And, harnessed like my horses, draw my coach;
And when ye stay, be lashed with whips of wire.
I'll have you learn to feed on provender
And in a stable lie upon the planks.
ORC. But, Tamburlaine, first thou shalt kneel to us,
And humbly crave a pardon for thy life.
K. OF TREB. The common soldiers of our mighty host
Shall bring thee bound unto the general's tent.
K. OF SOR. And all have jointly sworn thy cruel death,
Or bind thee in eternal torments' wrath.
TAMB. Well, sirs, diet yourselves; you know I shall have
occasion shortly to journey you.
CEL. See, father,
How Almeda the jailor looks upon us.
TAMB. Villain! traitor! damnèd fugitive!
I'll make thee wish the earth had swallowed thee,
See'st thou not death within my wrathful looks?
Go, villain, cast thee headlong from a rock,
Or rip thy bowels, and rend out thy heart
To appease my wrath! or else I'll torture thee,
Searing thy hateful flesh with burning irons
And drops of scalding lead, while all thy joints
Be racked and beat asunder with the wheel;
For, if thou liv'st, not any element
Shall shroud thee from the wrath of Tamburlaine.
CALL. Well, in despite of thee he shall be king.
Come, Almeda; receive this crown of me,
I here invest thee king of Ariadan
Bordering on Mare Roso,[1] near to Mecca.
ORC. What! Take it, man.
ALM. Good my lord, let me take it. [*To Tamburlaine.*
CALL. Dost thou ask him leave? Here; take it.
TAMB. Go to, sirrah, take your crown, and make up the half dozen.

---

1 The Red Sea.

So, sirrah, now you are a king, you must give arms.

ORC. So he shall, and wear thy head in his scutcheon.

TAMB. No; let him hang a bunch of keys on his standard to put him in remembrance he was a jailor, that when I take him, I may knock out his brains with them, and lock you in the stable, when you shall come sweating from my chariot.

K. OF TREB. Away; let us to the field, that the villain may be slain.

TAMB. Sirrah, prepare whips and bring my chariot to my tent, for as soon as the battle is done, I'll ride in triumph through the camp.

Enter THERIDAMAS, TECHELLES, *and their* Train.

How now, ye petty kings? Lo, here are bugs[2]
Will make the hair stand upright on your heads,
And cast your crowns in slavery at their feet.
Welcome, Theridamas and Techelles, both!
See ye this rout, and know ye this same king?

THER. Ay, my lord; he was Callapine's keeper.

TAMB. Well, now ye see he is a king; look to him,
Theridamas, when we are fighting, lest he hide his
crown as the foolish king of Persia did.

K. OF SOR. No, Tamburlaine; he shall not be put to that exigent, I warrant thee.

TAMB. You know not, sir—
But now, my followers and my loving friends,
Fight as you ever did, like conquerors,
The glory of this happy day is yours.
My stern aspèct shall make fair victory,
Hovering betwixt our armies, light on me
Loaden with laurel wreaths to crown us all.

TECH. I smile to think how, when this field is fought
And rich Natolia ours, our men shall sweat
With carrying pearl and treasure on their backs.

TAMB. You shall be princes all, immediately;
Come, fight ye Turks, or yield us victory.

ORC. No; we will meet thee, slavish Tamburlaine. [*Exeunt.*

2 Bugbears.

ACT THE FOURTH.

SCENE I.

Alarums within.—AMYRAS *and* CELEBINUS *issue from the tent where* CALYPHAS *sits asleep.*

AMY. Now in their glories shine the golden crowns
Of these proud Turks, much like so many suns
That half dismay the majesty of Heaven.
Now, brother, follow we our father's sword,
That flies with fury swifter than our thoughts,
And cuts down armies with his conquering wings.
CEL. Call forth our lazy brother from the tent,
For if my father miss him in the field,
Wrath, kindled in the furnace of his breast,
Will send a deadly lightning to his heart.
AMY. Brother, ho! what given so much to sleep!
You cannot leave it, when our enemies' drums
And rattling cannons thunder in our ears
Our proper ruin and our father's foil?
CAL. Away, ye fools! my father needs not me,
Nor you in faith, but that you will be thought
More childish-valorous than manly-wise.
If half our camp should sit and sleep with me,
My father were enough to scare the foe.
You do dishonour to his majesty,
To think our helps will do him any good.
AMY. What, dar'st thou then be absent from the field,
Knowing my father hates thy cowardice,
And oft hath warned thee to be still in field,
When he himself amidst the thickest troops
Beats down our foes, to flesh our taintless swords?
CAL. I know, sir, what it is to kill a man;
It works remorse of conscience in me;

I take no pleasure to be murderous,
Nor care for blood when wine will quench my thirst.
CEL. O cowardly boy! Fie! for shame come forth!
Thou dost dishonour manhood and thy house.
CAL. Go, go, tall[1] stripling, fight you for us both,
And take my other toward brother here,
For person like to prove a second Mars.
'Twill please my mind as well to hear you both
Have won a heap of honour in the field
And left your slender carcases behind,
As if I lay with you for company.
AMY. You will not go then?
CAL. You say true.
AMY. Were all the lofty mounts of Zona Mundi
That fill the midst of farthest Tartary
Turned into pearl and proffered for my stay,
I would not bide the fury of my father,
When, made a victor in these haughty arms,
He comes and finds his sons have had no shares
In all the honours he proposed for us.
CAL. Take you the honour, I will take my ease;
My wisdom shall excuse my cowardice.
I go into the field before I need!
[*Alarums.*—AMYRAS *and* CELEBINUS *run out.*
The bullets fly at random where they list;
And should I go and kill a thousand men,
I were as soon rewarded with a shot,
And sooner far than he that never fights;
And should I go and do no harm nor good,
I might have harm which all the good I have,
Joined with my father's crown, would never cure.
I'll to cards. Perdicas!

Enter PERDICAS.

PERDICAS. Here, my lord.
CAL. Come, thou and I will go to cards to drive away the time.
PERD. Content, my lord: but what shall we play for?
CAL. Who shall kiss the fairest of the Turk's concubines first, when my father hath conquered them.
PERD. Agreed, i' faith. [*They play.*

1 Brave, bold.

CAL. They say I am a coward, Perdicas, and I fear as little their taratantaras, their swords or their cannons, as I do a naked lady in a net of gold, and, for fear I should be afraid, would put it off and come to bed with me.

PERD. Such a fear, my lord, would never make ye retire.

CAL. I would my father would let me be put in the front of such a battle once to try my valour. [*Alarms within.*] What a coil they keep! I believe there will be some hurt done anon amongst them.

[*Exeunt.*

SCENE II.

Enter TAMBURLAINE, THERIDAMAS, TECHELLES, USUMCASANE, AMYRAS, *and* CELEBINUS, *leading in* ORCANES *and the* KINGS *of* JERUSALEM, TREBIZOND, *and* SORIA.

TAMB. See now, ye slaves, my children stoop[1] your pride,
And lead your bodies sheeplike to the sword.
Bring them, my boys, and tell me if the wars
Be not a life that may illustrate gods,
And tickle not your spirits with desire
Still to be trained in arms and chivalry?

AMY. Shall we let go these kings again, my lord,
To gather greater numbers 'gainst our power,
That they may say it is not chance doth this,
But matchless strength and magnanimity?

TAMB. No, no, Amyras; tempt not fortune so:
Cherish thy valour still with fresh supplies,
And glut it not with stale and daunted foes.
But where's this coward villain, not my son,
But traitor to my name and majesty?

[*He goes in and brings* CALYPHAS *out.*

Image of sloth and picture of a slave,
The obloquy and scorn of my renown!
How may my heart, thus firèd with mine eyes,
Wounded with shame and killed with discontent,
Shroud any thought may hold my striving hands
From martial justice on thy wretched soul?

THER. Yet pardon him, I pray your majesty.

TECH. and USUM. Let all of us entreat your highness' pardon.

---

1 Bend.

TAMB. Stand up, ye base, unworthy soldiers!
Know ye not yet the argument of arms?
AMY. Good my lord, let him be forgiven for once,
And we will force him to the field hereafter.
TAMB. Stand up, my boys, and I will teach ye arms,
And what the jealousy of wars must do.
O Samarcanda (where I breathèd first
And joyed the fire of this martial flesh),
Blush, blush, fair city, at thine honour's foil,[2]
And shame of nature, which Jaertis'[3] stream,
Embracing thee with deepest of his love,
Can never wash from thy distainèd brows!
Here, Jove, receive his fainting soul again;
A form not meet to give that subject essence
Whose matter is the flesh of Tamburlaine;
Wherein an incorporeal spirit moves,
Made of the mould whereof thyself consists,
Which makes me valiant, proud, ambitious,
Ready to levy power against thy throne,
That I might move the turning spheres of Heaven!
For earth and all this airy region
Cannot contain the state of Tamburlaine.
By Mahomet! thy mighty friend, I swear,
In sending to my issue such a soul,
Created of the massy dregs of earth,
The scum and tartar of the elements,
Wherein was neither courage, strength, or wit,
But folly, sloth, and damnèd idleness,
Thou hast procured a greater enemy
Than he that darted mountains at thy head,
Shaking the burthen mighty Atlas bears;
Whereat thou trembling hid'st thee in the air,
Clothed with a pitchy cloud for being seen:
And now, ye cankered curs of Asia,
That will not see the strength of Tamburlaine,
Although it shine as brightly as the sun;
Now you shall feel the strength of Tamburlaine,
And, by the state of his supremacy, [*Stabs* CALYPHAS.
Approve the difference 'twixt himself and you.

---

2 Soil.
3 Jaertis, *i.e.* Jaxartes, now the Ser-Daria in Bokhara.

ORC. Thou show'st the difference 'twixt ourselves and thee,
In this thy barbarous damnèd tyranny.
K. OF JER. Thy victories are grown so violent,
That shortly Heaven, filled with the meteors
Of blood and fire thy tyrannies have made,
Will pour down blood and fire on thy head,
Whose scalding drops will pierce thy seething brains,
And, with our bloods, revenge our bloods on thee.
TAMB. Villains! these terrors and these tyrannies
(If tyrannies war's justice ye repute),
I execute, enjoined me from above,
To scourge the pride of such as Heaven abhors;
Nor am I made arch-monarch of the world,
Crowned and invested by the hand of Jove
For deeds of bounty or nobility;
But since I exercise a greater name,
The scourge of God, and terror of the world,
I must apply myself to fit those terms,
In war, in blood, in death, in cruelty,
And plague such peasants as resist in me,
The power of Heaven's eternal majesty.
Theridamas, Techelles, and Casane,
Ransack the tents and the pavilions
Of these proud Turks, and take their concubines,
Making them bury this effeminate brat,
For not a common soldier shall defile
His manly fingers with so faint a boy.
Then bring those Turkish harlots to my tent,
And I'll dispose them as it likes me best;
Meanwhile, take him in.
SOLD. We will, my lord.

[*Exeunt with the body of* CALYPHAS.

K. OF JER. O damnèd monster! Nay, a fiend of hell,
Whose cruelties are not so harsh as thine,
Nor yet imposed with such a bitter hate!
ORC. Revenge it, Rhadamanth and Æacus,
And let your hates, extended in his pains,
Expel the hate wherewith he pains our souls.
K. OF TREB. May never day give virtue to his eyes,
Whose sight, composed of fury and of fire,
Doth send such stern affections to his heart.
K. OF SOR. May never spirit, vein, or artier, feed
The cursèd substance of that cruel heart!

But, wanting moisture and remorseful[4] blood,
Dry up with anger, and consume with heat.
TAMB. Well, bark, ye dogs; I'll bridle all your tongues,
And bind them close with bits of burnished steel,
Down to the channels of your hateful throats;
And, with the pains my rigour shall inflict,
I'll make ye roar, that earth may echo forth
The far resounding torments ye sustain:
As when an herd of lusty Cymbrian bulls
Run mourning round about the females' miss,[5]
And, stung with fury of their following,
Fill all the air with troublous bellowing;
I will, with engines never exercised,
Conquer, sack, and utterly consume
Your cities and your golden palaces;
And, with the flames that beat against the clouds,
Incense the Heavens, and make the stars to melt,
As if they were the tears of Mahomet,
For hot consumption of his country's pride;
And, till by vision or by speech I hear
Immortal Jove say "Cease, my Tamburlaine,"
I will persist, a terror to the world,
Making the meteors (that, like armèd men,
Are seen to march upon the towers of Heaven),
Run tilting round about the firmament,
And break their burning lances in the air,
For honour of my wondrous victories.
Come, bring them in to our pavilion. [*Exeunt.*

SCENE III.

OLYMPIA *discovered alone.*

OLYM. Distressed Olympia, whose weeping eyes,
Since thy arrival here behold no sun,
But closed within the compass of a tent
Have stained thy cheeks, and made thee look like death,
Devise some means to rid thee of thy life,
Rather than yield to his detested suit,

4 Compassionate.
5 Loss.

Whose drift is only to dishonour thee;
And since this earth, dewed with thy brinish tears,
Affords no herbs whose taste may poison thee,
Nor yet this air, beat often with thy sighs,
Contagious smells and vapours to infect thee,
Nor thy close cave a sword to murder thee;
Let this invention be the instrument.

Enter THERIDAMAS.

THER. Well met, Olympia; I sought thee in my tent,
But when I saw the place obscure and dark,
Which with thy beauty thou was't wont to light,
Enraged, I ran about the fields for thee,
Supposing amorous Jove had sent his son,
The wingèd Hermes, to convey thee hence;
But now I find thee, and that fear is past.
Tell me, Olympia, wilt thou grant my suit?
OLYM. My lord and husband's death, with my sweet son's
(With whom I buried all affections
Save grief and sorrow, which torment my heart),
Forbids my mind to entertain a thought
That tends to love, but meditate on death,
A fitter subject for a pensive soul.
THER. Olympia, pity him, in whom thy looks
Have greater operation and more force
Than Cynthia's in the watery wilderness,
For with thy view my joys are at the full,
And ebb again as thou departest from me.
OLYM. Ah, pity me, my lord! and draw your sword,
Making a passage for my troubled soul,
Which beats against this prison to get out,
And meet my husband and my loving son.
THER. Nothing but still thy husband and thy son!
Leave this, my love, and listen more to me.
Thou shalt be stately queen of fair Argier;
And clothed in costly cloth of massy gold,
Upon the marble turrets of my court
Sit like to Venus in her chair of state,
Commanding all thy princely eye desires;
And I will cast off arms to sit with thee,
Spending my life in sweet discourse of love.
OLYM. No such discourse is pleasant in mine ears,
But that where every period ends with death,

And every line begins with death again.
I cannot love, to be an emperess.

THER. Nay, lady, then, if nothing will prevail,
I'll use some other means to make you yield:
Such is the sudden fury of my love,
I must and will be pleased, and you shall yield:
Come to the tent again.

OLYM. Stay now, my lord; and, will you save my honour,
I'll give your grace a present of such price,
As all the world cannot afford the like.

THER. What is it?

OLYM. An ointment which a cunning alchymist,
Distillèd from the purest balsamum
And simplest extracts of all minerals,
In which the essential form of marble stone,
Tempered by science metaphysical,
And spells of magic from the mouths of spirits,
With which if you but 'noint your tender skin,
Nor pistols, sword, nor lance, can pierce your flesh.

THER. Why, madam, think you to mock me thus palpably?

OLYM. To prove it, I will 'noint my naked throat,
Which, when you stab, look on your weapon's point,
And you shall see't rebated[6] with the blow.

THER. Why gave you not your husband some of it,
If you loved him, and it so precious?

OLYMP. My purpose was, my lord, to spend it so.
But was prevented by his sudden end;
And for a present, easy proof thereof,
That I dissemble not, try it on me.

THER. I will, Olympia, and will keep it for
The richest present of this eastern world.

[She anoints her throat.

OLYM. Now stab, my lord, and mark your weapon's point,
That will be blunted if the blow be great.

THER. Here then, Olympia. *[Stabs her.*
What, have I slain her! Villain, stab thyself;
Cut off this arm that murderèd my love,
In whom the learnèd rabbis of this age
Might find as many wondrous miracles
As in the theoria of the world.

---

6 Blunted.

Now hell is fairer than Elysium;
A greater lamp than that bright eye of Heaven,
From whence the stars do borrow all their light,
Wanders about the black circumference;
And now the damnèd souls are free from pain,
For every Fury gazeth on her looks;
Infernal Dis is courting of my love,
Inventing masks and stately shows for her,
Opening the doors of his rich treasury
To entertain this queen of chastity;
Whose body shall be tombed with all the pomp
The treasure of my kingdom may afford.

[*Exit, with the body.*

Scene IV.

Enter Tamburlaine *drawn in his chariot by the* Kings *of* Trebizond *and* Soria, *with bits in their mouths: in his right hand he has a whip with which he scourgeth them, while his left hand holds the reins; then come* Techelles, Theridamas, Usumcasane, Amyras, *and* Celebinus *with the* Kings *of* Natolia *and* Jerusalem, *led by five or six common* Soldiers.

Tamb. Holla, ye pampered jades of Asia!
What! can ye draw but twenty miles a day,
And have so proud a chariot at your heels,
And such a coachman as great Tamburlaine,
But from Asphaltis, where I conquered you,
To Byron here, where thus I honour you!
The horse that guide the golden eye of Heaven,
And blow the morning from their nosterils,
Making their fiery gait above the clouds,
Are not so honoured in their governor,
As you, ye slaves, in mighty Tamburlaine.
The headstrong jades of Thrace Alcides tamed,
That King Egeus fed with human flesh,
And made so wanton that they knew their strengths,
Were not subdued with valour more divine
Than you by this unconquered arm of mine.
To make you fierce, and fit my appetite,
You shall be fed with flesh as raw as blood,
And drink in pails the strongest muscadel;

If you can live with it, then live, and draw
My chariot swifter than the racking[1] clouds;
If not, then die like beasts, and fit for naught
But perches for the black and fatal ravens.
Thus am I right the scourge of highest Jove;
And see the figure of my dignity
By which I hold my name and majesty!

AMY. Let me have coach, my lord, that I may ride,
And thus be drawn by these two idle kings.

TAMB. Thy youth forbids such ease, my kingly boy;
They shall to-morrow draw my chariot,
While these their fellow-kings may be refreshed.

ORC. O thou that sway'st the region under earth,
And art a king as absolute as Jove,
Come as thou didst in fruitful Sicily,
Surveying all the glories of the land,
And as thou took'st the fair Proserpina,
Joying the fruit of Ceres' garden-plot,
For love, for honour, and to make her queen,
So for just hate, for shame, and to subdue
This proud contemner of thy dreadful power,
Come once in fury and survey his pride,
Haling him headlong to the lowest hell.

THER. Your majesty must get some bits for these,
To bridle their contemptuous, cursing tongues,
That, like unruly, never-broken jades,
Break through the hedges of their hateful mouths,
And pass their fixèd bounds exceedingly.

TECH. Nay, we will break the hedges of their mouths,
And pull their kicking colts out of their pastures.

USUM. Your majesty already hath devised
A mean, as fit as may be, to restrain
These coltish coach-horse tongues from blasphemy.

CEL. How like you that, sir king? Why speak you not?

K. OF JER. Ah, cruel brat, sprung from a tyrant's loins!
How like his cursèd father he begins
To practise taunts and bitter tyrannies!

TAMB. Ay, Turk, I tell thee, this same boy is he
That must (advanced in higher pomp than this)
Rifle the kingdoms I shall leave unsacked,

1 Scudding.

If Jove, esteeming me too good for earth,
Raise me to match the fair Aldeboran,
Above the threefold astracism of Heaven,
Before I conquer all the triple world.
Now, fetch me out the Turkish concubines;
I will prefer them for the funeral
They have bestowed on my abortive son.

[*The* Concubines *are brought in.*

Where are my common soldiers now, that fought
So lion-like upon Asphaltis' plains?

SOLD. Here, my lord.

TAMB. Hold ye, tall[2] soldiers, take ye queens apiece—
I mean such queens as were kings' concubines—
Take them; divide them, and their jewels too,
And let them equally serve all your turns.

SOLD. We thank you.

TAMB. Brawl not, I warn you, for your lechery:
For every man that so offends shall die.

ORC. Injurious tyrant, wilt thou so defame
The hateful fortunes of thy victory,
To exercise upon such guiltless dames
The violence of thy common soldiers' lust?

TAMB. Live continent then, ye slaves, and meet not me
With troops of harlots at your slothful heels.

CON. O pity us, my lord, and save our honours.

TAMB. Are ye not gone, ye villains, with your spoils?

[*They run away with the* Concubines.

K. OF JER. O merciless, infernal cruelty!

TAMB. Save your honours! 'Twere but time indeed,
Lost long before ye knew what honour meant.

THER. It seems they meant to conquer us, my lord,
And make us jesting pageants for their trulls.

TAMB. And now themselves shall make our pageants,
And common soldiers jest with all their trulls.
Let them take pleasure soundly in their spoils,
Till we prepare our march to Babylon,
Whither we next make expedition.

TECH. Let us not be idle then, my lord,
But presently be prest[3] to conquer it.

TAMB. We will, Techelles. Forward then, ye jades.

---

2 Brave.

3 Ready.

Now crouch, ye kings of greatest Asia,
And tremble when ye hear this scourge will come
That whips down cities and controlleth crowns,
Adding their wealth and treasure to my store.
The Euxine sea, north to Natolia;
The Terrene, west; the Caspian, north-north-east;
And on the south, Sinus Arabicus;
Shall all be loaden with the martial spoils
We will convey with us to Persia.
Then shall my native city, Samarcanda,
And crystal waves of fresh Jaertis' stream,
The pride and beauty of her princely seat,
Be famous through the furthest continents,
For there my palace-royal shall be placed,
Whose shining turrets shall dismay the Heavens,
And cast the fame of Ilion's tower to hell.
Thorough the streets with troops of conquered kings,
I'll ride in golden armour like the sun;
And in my helm a triple plume shall spring,
Spangled with diamonds, dancing in the air,
To note me emperor of the threefold world,
Like to an almond tree y-mounted high
Upon the lofty and celestial mount
Of ever-green Selinus, quaintly decked
With blooms more white than Erycina's brows,
Whose tender blossoms tremble every one,
At every little breath through Heaven is blown.
Then in my coach, like Saturn's royal son
Mounted, his shining chariot gilt with fire,
And drawn with princely eagles through the path
Paved with bright crystal and enchased with stars,
When all the gods stand gazing at his pomp,
So will I ride through Samarcanda streets,
Until my soul, dissevered from this flesh,
Shall mount the milk-white way, and meet him there.
To Babylon, my lords; to Babylon! [*Exeunt.*

ACT FIVE.

SCENE I.

Enter the GOVERNOR *of* BABYLON, MAXIMUS, *and others upon the walls.*

GOV. What saith Maximus?
MAX. My lord, the breach the enemy hath made
Gives such assurance of our overthrow
That little hope is left to save our lives,
Or hold our city from the conqueror's hands.
Then hang out flags, my lord, of humble truce,
And satisfy the people's general prayers,
That Tamburlaine's intolerable wrath
May be suppressed by our submission.
GOV. Villain, respects thou more thy slavish life
Than honour of thy country or thy name?
Is not my life and state as dear to me,
The city, and my native country's weal,
As anything of price with thy conceit?
Have we not hope, for all our battered walls,
To live secure and keep his forces out,
When this our famous lake of Limnasphaltis
Makes walls afresh with everything that falls
Into the liquid substance of his stream,
More strong than are the gates of death or hell?
What faintness should dismay our courages
When we are thus defenced against our foes,
And have no terror but his threatening looks.

Enter above a Citizen, *who kneels to the* GOVERNOR.

CIT. My lord, if ever you did deed of ruth,
And now will work a refuge for our lives,
Offer submission, hang up flags of truce,
That Tamburlaine may pity our distress,
And use us like a loving conqueror.
Though this be held his last day's dreadful siege,
Wherein he spareth neither man nor child,
Yet are there Christians of Georgia here,
Whose state was ever pitied and relieved,
Would get his pardon if your grace would send.

GOV. How is my soul environèd with cares!
And this eternized city, Babylon,
Filled with a pack of faint-heart fugitives
That thus entreat their shame and servitude!

Enter another Citizen.

2nd CIT. My lord, if ever you will win our hearts,
Yield up the town and save our wives and children;
For I will cast myself from off these walls
Or die some death of quickest violence
Before I bide the wrath of Tamburlaine.

GOV. Villains, cowards, traitors to our state!
Fall to the earth and pierce the pit of hell,
That legions of tormenting spirits may vex
Your slavish bosoms with continual pains!
I care not, nor the town will never yield,
As long as any life is in my breast.

Enter THERIDAMAS, TECHELLES, *with* Soldiers.

THER. Thou desperate governor of Babylon,
To save thy life, and us a little labour,
Yield speedily the city to our hands,
Or else be sure thou shalt be forced with pains,
More exquisite than ever traitor felt.

GOV. Tyrant! I turn the traitor in thy throat,
And will defend it in despite of thee.—
Call up the soldiers to defend these walls!

TECH. Yield, foolish governor; we offer more
Than ever yet we did to such proud slaves
As durst resist us till our third day's siege.
Thou seest us prest to give the last assault,
And that shall bide no more regard of parley.

GOV. Assault and spare not; we will never yield.

[*Alarms: and they scale the walls.*

Enter TAMBURLAINE *drawn in his chariot by the* KINGS *of* TREBIZOND *and* SORIA; AMYRAS, CELEBINUS, *and* USUMCASANE; *with the two spare* KINGS *of* Natolia *and* Jerusalem *led by* Soldiers, *and others.*

TAMB. The stately buildings of fair Babylon,
Whose lofty pillars, higher than the clouds,
Were wont to guide the seaman in the deep,
Being carried thither by the cannon's force,
Now fill the mouth of Limnasphaltis' lake
And make a bridge unto the battered walls.
Where Belus, Ninus, and great Alexander
Have rode in triumph, triumphs Tamburlaine,
Whose chariot wheels have burst the Assyrians' bones,
Drawn with these kings on heaps of carcases.
Now in the place where fair Semiramis,
Courted by kings and peers of Asia,
Hath trod the measures,[1] do my soldiers march;
And in the streets, where brave Assyrian dames
Have rid in pomp like rich Saturnia,
With furious words and frowning visages
My horsemen brandish their unruly blades.

Enter THERIDAMAS *and* TECHELLES, *bringing in the* GOVERNOR *of* BABYLON.

Who have ye there, my lords?
THER. The sturdy governor of Babylon,
That made us all the labour for the town,
And used such slender reckoning of your majesty.
TAMB. Go, bind the villain; he shall hang in chains
Upon the ruins of this conquered town.
Sirrah, the view of our vermilion tents
(Which threatened more than if the region
Next underneath the element of fire
Were full of comets and of blazing stars,
Whose flaming trains should reach down to the earth),
Could not affright you; no, nor I myself,
The wrathful messenger of mighty Jove,
That with his sword hath quailed all earthly kings,
Could not persuade you to submission,
But still the ports[2] were shut; villain! I say,

---

1 A slow stately dance.
2 Gates

Should I but touch the rusty gates of hell,
The triple-headed Cerberus would howl
And make black Jove to crouch and kneel to me;
But I have sent volleys of shot to you,
Yet could not enter till the breach was made.

GOV. Nor, if my body could have stopt the breach,
Should'st thou have entered, cruel Tamburlaine.
'Tis not thy bloody tents can make me yield,
Nor yet thyself, the anger of the Highest,
For though thy cannon shook the city walls,
My heart did never quake, or courage faint.

TAMB. Well, now I'll make it quake; go, draw him up,
Hang him in chains upon the city walls,
And let my soldiers shoot the slave to death.

GOV. Vile monster! born of some infernal hag,
And sent from hell to tyrannise on earth,
Do all thy worst; nor death, nor Tamburlaine,
Torture, nor pain, can daunt my dreadless mind.

TAMB. Up with him, then; his body shall be scared.

GOV. But, Tamburlaine, in Limnasphaltis' lake
There lies more gold than Babylon is worth,
Which when the city was besieged, I hid.
Save but my life and I will give it thee.

TAMB. Then for all your valour, you would save your life?
Whereabout lies it?

GOV. Under a hollow bank, right opposite
Against the western gate of Babylon.

TAMB. Go thither, some of you, and take his gold;—
[*Exeunt some of the* Attendants.
The rest—forward with execution!
Away with him hence, let him speak no more.
I think I make your courage something quail.
[*Exeunt other* Attendants, *with the* GOVERNOR *of* BABYLON
When this is done, we'll march from Babylon,
And make our greatest haste to Persia.
These jades are broken-winded and half tired,
Unharness them, and let me have fresh horse.
[*Attendants unharness the* KINGS *of* TREBIZOND *and* SORIA
So, now their best is done to honour me,
Take them and hang them both up presently.

K. OF TREB. Vile tyrant! barbarous bloody Tamburlaine!

TAMB. Take them away, Theridamas; see them dispatched.

THER. I will, my lord.
[*Exit with the* KINGS *of* TREBIZON *and* SORIA.

TAMB. Come, Asian viceroys; to your tasks awhile,
And take such fortune as your fellows felt.
ORC. First let thy Scythian horse tear both our limbs.
Rather than we should draw thy chariot,
And like base slaves abject our princely minds
To vile and ignominious servitude.
K. OF JER. Rather lend me thy weapon, Tamburlaine,
That I may sheathe it in this breast of mine.
A thousand deaths could not torment our hearts
More than the thought of this doth vex our souls.
AMY. They will talk still, my lord, if you don't bridle them.
TAMB. Bridle them, and let me to my coach.
[*They bridle the* KINGS *of* NATOLIA *and* JERUSALEM *and harness them to the chariot. The* GOVERNOR *is seen hanging in chains on the walls.*

Re-enter THERIDAMAS.

AMY. See now, my lord, how brave the captain hangs.
TAMB. 'Tis brave indeed my boy; well done.
Shoot first, my lord, and then the rest shall follow.
THER. Then have at him to begin withal.
[THERIDAMAS *shoots at the* GOVERNOR.
GOV. Yet save my life, and let this wound appease
The mortal fury of great Tamburlaine.
TAMB. No, though Asphaltis' lake were liquid gold,
And offered me as ransom for thy life,
Yet should'st thou die. Shoot at him all at once.
[*They shoot.*
So, now he hangs like Bagdet's governor,
Having as many bullets in his flesh
As there be breaches in her battered wall.
Go now, and bind the burghers hand and foot,
And cast them headlong in the city's lake.
Tartars and Persians shall inhabit there,
And, to command the city, I will build
A lofty citadel that all Africa,
Which hath been subject to the Persian king,
Shall pay me tribute for in Babylon.
TECH. What shall be done with their wives and children, my lord?
TAMB. Techelles, drown them all, man, woman, and child.
Leave not a Babylonian in the town.
TECH. I will about it straight. Come, soldiers. [*Exit with* Soldiers.
TAMB. Now, Casane, where's the Turkish Alcoran,

And all the heaps of superstitious books
Found in the temples of that Mahomet,
Whom I have thought a god? They shall be burnt.

USUM. Here they are, my lord.

TAMB. Well said; let there be a fire presently. [*They light a fire.*
In vain, I see, men worship Mahomet:
My sword hath sent millions of Turks to hell,
Slain all his priests, his kinsmen, and his friends,
And yet I live untouched by Mahomet.
There is a God, full of revenging wrath,
From whom the thunder and the lightning breaks,
Whose scourge I am, and him will I obey:
So, Casane, fling them in the fire. [*They burn the books.*
Now, Mahomet, if thou have any power,
Come down thyself and work a miracle:
Thou art not worthy to be worshippèd,
That suffers flame of fire to burn the writ
Wherein the sum of thy religion rests.
Why send'st thou not a furious whirlwind down
To blow thy Alcoran up to thy throne,
Where men report thou sit'st by God himself?
Or vengeance on the head of Tamburlaine
That shakes his sword against thy majesty,
And spurns the abstracts of thy foolish laws?
Well, soldiers, Mahomet remains in hell;
He cannot hear the voice of Tamburlaine;
Seek out another Godhead to adore,
The God that sits in Heaven, if any God;
For he is God alone, and none but he.

Re-enter TECHELLES.

TECH. I have fulfilled your highness' will, my lord.
Thousands of men, drowned in Asphaltis' lake,
Have make the waters swell above the banks,
And fishes, fed by human carcases,
Amazed, swim up and down upon the waves,
As when they swallow assafœtida,
Which makes them fleet[3] aloft and gape for air.

TAMB. Well then, my friendly lords, what now remains,
But that we leave sufficient garrison,

3 Float.

And presently depart to Persia
To triumph after all our victories?
THER. Ay, good my lord; let us in haste to Persia,
And let this captain be removed the walls
To some high hill about the city here.
TAMB. Let it be so; about it, soldiers;
But stay; I feel myself distempered suddenly.
TECH. What is it dares distemper Tamburlaine?
TAMB. Something, Techelles; but I know not what—
But, forth, ye vassals! whatsoe'er it be,
Sickness or death can never conquer me. [*Exeunt.*

SCENE II.

Enter CALLAPINE, *the* KING *of* AMASIA, *a* Captain *and* Soldiers, *with drums and trumpets.*

CALL. King of Amasia, now our mighty host
Marcheth in Asia Major where the streams
Of Euphrates and Tigris swiftly run,
And here may we behold great Babylon
Circled about with Limnasphaltis' lake
Where Tamburlaine with all his army lies,
Which being faint and weary with the siege,
We may lie ready to encounter him
Before his host be full from Babylon,
And so revenge our latest grievous loss,
If God or Mahomet send any aid.
K. OF AMA. Doubt not, my lord, but we shall conquer him.
The monster that hath drunk a sea of blood,
And yet gapes still for more to quench his thirst,
Our Turkish swords shall headlong send to hell,
And that vile carcase drawn by warlike kings
The fowls shall eat; for never sepulchre
Shall grace this base-born tyrant Tamburlaine.
CALL. When I record[1] my parents' slavish life,
Their cruel death, mine own captivity,
My viceroy's bondage under Tamburlaine,
Methinks I could sustain a thousand deaths
To be revenged of all his villany.

---

1 Recall.

Ah, sacred Mahomet! thou that hast seen
Millions of Turks perish by Tamburlaine,
Kingdoms made waste, brave cities sacked and burnt,
And but one host is left to honour thee,
Aid thy obedient servant, Callapine,
And make him after all these overthrows
To triumph over cursèd Tamburlaine.

K. OF AMA. Fear not, my lord; I see great Mahomet
Clothèd in purple clouds, and on his head
A chaplet brighter than Apollo's crown,
Marching about the air with armèd men
To join with you against this Tamburlaine.

CAPT. Renownèd general, mighty Callapine,
Though God himself and holy Mahomet
Should come in person to resist your power,
Yet might your mighty host encounter all,
And pull proud Tamburlaine upon his knees
To sue for mercy at your highness' feet.

CALL. Captain, the force of Tamburlaine is great,
His fortune greater, and the victories
Wherewith he hath so sore dismayed the world
Are greatest to discourage all our drifts;
Yet when the pride of Cynthia is at full,
She wanes again, and so shall his, I hope;
For we have here the chief selected men
Of twenty several kingdoms at the least;
Nor ploughman, priest, nor merchant, stays at home;
All Turkey is in arms with Callapine;
And never will we sunder camps and arms
Before himself or his be conquerèd.
This is the time that must eternise me
For conquering the tyrant of the world.
Come, soldiers, let us lie in wait for him,
And if we find him absent from his camp,
Or that it be rejoined again at full,
Assail it and be sure of victory. [*Exeunt.*

SCENE III.

Enter THERIDAMAS, TECHELLES, *and* USUMCASANE.

THER. Weep, heavens, and vanish into liquid tears!
Fall, stars that govern his nativity,

And summon all the shining lamps of Heaven
To cast their bootless fires to the earth,
And shed their feeble influence in the air;
Muffle your beauties with eternal clouds,
For Hell and Darkness pitch their pitchy tents,
And Death with armies of Cimmerian spirits
Gives battle 'gainst the heart of Tamburlaine!
Now in defiance of that wonted love
Your sacred virtues poured upon his throne
And made his state an honour to the Heavens,
These cowards invisible assail his soul,
And threaten conquest on our sovereign;
But if he die your glories are disgraced;
Earth droops and says that hell in Heaven is placed.

TECH. O then, ye powers that sway eternal seats
And guide this massy substance of the earth,
If you retain desert of holiness
As your supreme estates instruct our thoughts,
Be not inconstant, careless of your fame,—
Bear not the burthen of your enemies' joys
Triumphing in his fall whom you advanced,
But as his birth, life, health, and majesty
Were strangely blest and governèd by Heaven,
So honour, Heaven, (till Heaven dissolvèd be)
His birth, his life, his health, and majesty!

USUM. Blush, Heaven, to lose the honour of thy name!
To see thy footstool set upon thy head!
And let no baseness in thy haughty breast
Sustain a shame of such inexcellence,
To see the devils mount in angels' thrones,
And angels dive into the pools of hell!
And though they think their painful date is out,
And that their power is puissant as Jove's,
Which makes them manage arms against thy state,
Yet make them feel the strength of Tamburlaine,
(Thy instrument and note of majesty),
Is greater far than they can thus subdue:
For if he die thy glory is disgraced;
Earth droops and says that hell in Heaven is placed.

Enter TAMBURLAINE, *drawn in his chariot by the captive* Kings *as before;* AMYRAS, CELEBINUS, *and* Physicians.

TAMB. What daring god torments my body thus,
And seeks to conquer mighty Tamburlaine?
Shall sickness prove me now to be a man,
That have been termed the terror of the world?
Techelles and the rest, come, take your swords,
And threaten him whose hand afflicts my soul.
Come, let us march against the powers of Heaven,
And set black streamers in the firmament,
To signify the slaughter of the gods.
Ah, friends, what shall I do? I cannot stand.
Come carry me to war against the gods
That thus envy the health of Tamburlaine.
THER. Ah, good my lord, leave these impatient words,
Which add much danger to your malady.
TAMB. Why, shall I sit and languish in this pain?
No, strike the drums, and in revenge of this,
Come, let us charge our spears and pierce his breast,
Whose shoulders bear the axis of the world,
That, if I perish, Heaven and earth may fade.
Theridamas, haste to the court of Jove,
Will him to send Apollo hither straight,
To cure me, or I'll fetch him down myself.
TECH. Sit still, my gracious lord; this grief will cease,
And cannot last, it is so violent.
TAMB. Not last, Techelles?—No! for I shall die.
See, where my slave, the ugly monster, Death,
Shaking and quivering, pale and wan for fear,
Stands aiming at me with his murdering dart,
Who flies away at every glance I give,
And, when I look away, comes stealing on.
Villain, away, and hie thee to the field!
I and mine army come to load thy back
With souls of thousand mangled carcases.
Look, where he goes; but see, he comes again,
Because I stay: Techelles, let us march
And weary Death with bearing souls to hell.
1ST PHY. Pleaseth your majesty to drink this potion,
Which will abate the fury of your fit,
And cause some milder spirits govern you.
TAMB. Tell me what think you of my sickness now?
1ST PHY. I viewed your urine, and the hypostasis
Thick and obscure, doth make your danger great;

Your veins are full of accidental heat,
Whereby the moisture of your blood is dried.
The humidum and calor, which some hold
Is not a parcel of the elements,
But of a substance more divine and pure,
Is almost clean extinguishèd and spent;
Which, being the cause of life, imports your death.
Besides, my lord, this day is critical,
Dangerous to those whose crisis is as yours;
Your artiers, which alongst the veins convey
The lively spirits which the heart engenders,
Are parched and void of spirits, that the soul,
Wanting those organons by which it moves,
Cannot endure, by argument of art.
Yet, if your majesty may escape this day,
No doubt but you shall soon recover all.

TAMB. Then will I comfort all my vital parts,
And live, in spite of death, above a day. [*Alarms within.*

Enter Messenger.

MES. My lord, young Callapine, that lately fled from your majesty, hath now gathered a fresh army, and hearing your absence in the field, offers to set upon us presently.

TAMB. See, my physicians now, how Jove hath sent
A present medicine to recure my pain.
My looks shall make them fly, and might I follow,
There should not one of all the villain's power
Live to give offer of another fight.

USUM. I joy, my lord, your highness is so strong,
That can endure so well your royal presence,
Which only will dismay the enemy.

TAMB. I know it will, Casane. Draw, you slaves;
In spite of death, I will go show my face.

[*Alarums.—Exit* TAMBURLAINE *and the rest, with the exception of the* Physicians. *They all presently re-enter.*

TAMB. Thus are the villain cowards fled for fear,
Like summer's vapours vanished by the sun;
And could I but awhile pursue the field,
That Callapine should be my slave again.
But I perceive my martial strength is spent.
In vain I strive and rail against those powers,
That mean to invest me in a higher throne,

As much too high for this disdainful earth.
Give me a map; then let me see how much
Is left for me to conquer all the world,
That these, my boys, may finish all my wants.
[*One brings a map.*
Here I began to march towards Persia,
Along Armenia and the Caspian Sea,
And thence unto Bithynia, where I took
The Turk and his great Empress prisoners.
Then marched I into Egypt and Arabia,
And here, not far from Alexandria,
Whereas the Terrene and the Red Sea meet,
Being distant less than full a hundred leagues,
I meant to cut a channel to them both,
That men might quickly sail to India.
From thence to Nubia near Borno lake,
And so along the Æthiopian sea,
Cutting the Tropic line of Capricorn,
I conquered all as far as Zanzibar.
Then, by the northern part of Africa,
I came at last to Græcia, and from thence
To Asia, where I stay against my will;
Which is from Scythia, where I first began,
Backwards and forwards near five thousand leagues.
Look here, my boys; see what a world of ground
Lies westward from the midst of Cancer's line,
Unto the rising of this earthly globe:
Whereas the sun, declining from our sight,
Begins the day with our Antipodes!
And shall I die, and this unconquerèd?
Lo, here, my sons, are all the golden mines,
Inestimable drugs and precious stones,
More worth than Asia and the world beside;
And from the Antarctic Pole eastward behold
As much more land, which never was descried,
Wherein are rocks of pearl that shine as bright
As all the lamps that beautify the sky!
And shall I die, and this unconquerèd?
Here, lovely boys; what death forbids my life,
That let your lives command in spite of death.

AMY. Alas, my lord, how should our bleeding hearts,
Wounded and broken with your highness' grief,
Retain a thought of joy or spark of life?

Your soul gives essence to our wretched subjects,
Whose matter is incorporate in your flesh.

CEL. Your pains do pierce our souls; no hope survives,
For by your life we entertain our lives.

TAMB. But, sons, this subject, not of force enough
To hold the fiery spirit it contains,
Must part, imparting his impressions
By equal portions into both your breasts;
My flesh, divided in your precious shapes,
Shall still retain my spirit, though I die,
And live in all your seeds immortally.
Then now remove me, that I may resign
My place and proper title to my son.
First, take my scourge and my imperial crown,
And mount my royal chariot of estate,
That I may see thee crowned before I die.
Help me, my lords, to make my last remove.

[*They lift him from the chariot.*

THER. A woful change, my lord, that daunts our thoughts,
More than the ruin of our proper souls!

TAMB. Sit up, my son, let me see how well
Thou wilt become thy father's majesty.

AMY. With what a flinty bosom should I joy
The breath of life and burthen of my soul,
If not resolved into resolvèd pains,
My body's mortifièd lineaments
Should exercise the motions of my heart,
Pierced with the joy of any dignity!
O father! if the unrelenting ears
Of death and hell be shut against my prayers,
And that the spiteful influence of Heaven,
Deny my soul fruition of her joy;
How should I step, or stir my hateful feet
Against the inward powers of my heart,
Leading a life that only strives to die,
And plead in vain unpleasing sovereignty?

TAMB. Let not thy love exceed thine honour, son,
Nor bar thy mind that magnanimity
That nobly must admit necessity.
Sit up, my boy, and with those silken reins
Bridle the steelèd stomachs of those jades.

THER. My lord, you must obey his majesty,
Since fate commands and proud necessity.

AMY. Heavens witness me with what a broken heart
And damnèd spirit I ascend this seat,
And send my soul, before my father die,
His anguish and his burning agony!
[*They crown* AMYRAS.

TAMB. Now fetch the hearse of fair Zenocrate;
Let it be placed by this my fatal chair,
And serve as parcel of my funeral.

USUM. Then feels your majesty no sovereign ease,
Nor may our hearts, all drowned in tears of blood,
Joy any hope of your recovery?

TAMB. Casane, no; the monarch of the earth,
And eyeless monster that torments my soul,
Cannot behold the tears ye shed for me,
And therefore still augments his cruelty.

TECH. Then let some God oppose his holy power
Against the wrath and tyranny of Death,
That his tear-thirsty and unquenchèd hate
May be upon himself reverberate!
[*They bring in the hearse of* ZENOCRATE.

TAMB. Now eyes enjoy your latest benefit,
And when my soul hath virtue of your sight,
Pierce through the coffin and the sheet of gold,
And glut your longings with a heaven of joy.
So reign, my son; scourge and control those slaves,
Guiding thy chariot with thy father's hand.
As precious is the charge thou undertakest
As that which Clymene's brain-sick son did guide,
When wandering Phœbe's ivory cheeks were scorched,
And all the earth, like Ætna, breathing fire;
Be warned by him, then; learn with awful eye
To sway a throne as dangerous as his;
For if thy body thrive not full of thoughts
As pure and fiery as Phyteus'[1] beams,
The nature of these proud rebelling jades
Will take occasion by the slenderest hair,
And draw thee piecemeal like Hippolitus,
Through rocks more steep and sharp than Caspian clifts.
The nature of thy chariot will not bear
A guide of baser temper than myself,

1 Probably a form of "Pythius."

More than Heaven's coach the pride of Phaeton.
Farewell, my boys; my dearest friends, farewell!
My body feels, my soul doth weep to see
Your sweet desires deprived my company,
For Tamburlaine, the scourge of God, must die. *[He dies.*

AMY. Meet Heaven and Earth, and here let all things end,
For Earth hath spent the pride of all her fruit,
And Heaven consumed his choicest living fire.
Let Earth and Heaven his timeless[2] death deplore,
For both their worths will equal him no more.

2 Untimely.